POLITICAL THOUGHT

in Canada

POLITICAL THOUGHT
in Canada

An Intellectual History

KATHERINE FIERLBECK

broadview press

Library and Archives Canada Cataloguing in Publication

Fierlbeck, Katherine

    Political thought in Canada : an intellectual history / Katherine Fierlbeck.

Includes bibliographical references and index.
ISBN 1-55111-711-8

    1. Political science—Canada—History. 2. Political culture—Canada—History. 3. Canada—Politics and government. I. Title.

JA84.C3F53 2006   320'.0971'09   C2006-900171-5

Broadview Press is an independent, international publishing house, incorporated in 1985. Broadview believes in shared ownership, both with its employees and with the general public; since the year 2000 Broadview shares have traded publicly on the Toronto Venture Exchange under the symbol BDP.

We welcome comments and suggestions regarding any aspect of our publications–please feel free to contact us at the addresses below or at broadview@broadviewpress.com / www.broadviewpress.com

North America
PO Box 1243, Peterborough, Ontario, Canada K9J 7H5
Tel: (705) 743-8990; Fax: (705) 743-8353
email: customerservice@broadviewpress.com
3576 California Road, PO Box 1015, Orchard Park, NY, USA 14127

UK, Ireland, and continental Europe
NBN International
Estover Road
Plymouth PL6 7PY UK
Tel: 44 (0) 1752 202 300
Fax: 44 (0) 1752 202 330
email: enquiries@nbninternational.com

Australia and New Zealand
UNIREPS, University of New South Wales
Sydney, NSW, 2052
Australia
Tel: 61 2 9664 0999; Fax: 61 2 9664 5420
email: info.press@unsw.edu.au

Broadview Press gratefully acknowledges the financial support of the Government of Canada through the Book Publishing Industry Development Program for our publishing activities.

PRINTED IN CANADA

This book is dedicated to my children,
so they may shape their future with an understanding of their past.

CONTENTS

PREFACE

Why, mused a friend, have Canadians not made a point of "traditionalizing" their political thought? She pointed out that Americans, concerned with gathering their citizens around tradition (and, specifically, around the regular iteration of republican principles), study political thought in a systematic national-historical way that Canadians manifestly do not. One might respond that this is not entirely accurate, that Canadians do have a particular tradition of political thought, even if it is not promoted as enthusiastically as is the canon of republican thought in the United States. The Canadian political tradition, one might suggest, is based upon a Tory sensibility: continuity with history, organic collectivity, and a sense of moderation are some of the qualities represented by the Tory tradition. Canada's comfort with Tory principles, as Gad Horowitz famously argued, facilitated the acceptance of socialism in Canada. The view of Canada as a "community of communities" is informed by its Tory past. Canada's health care system, its gun control legislation, and its international multilateralist approach are based on Tory values. And so on.

But there are some problems with this national myth. One is that we rarely use the adjective "Tory" now (except in the rare instance of having to defend the existence of a national tradition of political thought). Another is that it is becoming increasingly difficult to find undergraduates who understand what is meant by the term "Tory". It is even rarer to find a living person who actually espouses such principles. And, since the amalgamation of the Conservative and Reform parties, even journalists doubt the accuracy of referring to members of the new party as "Tories."

Historians themselves might add that "Toryism" never really existed in the form imputed to it by contemporary theorists. Edmund Burke is commonly used as a reference point for the definition of Toryism, although, for all his reverence of the ill-fated

French monarchy, Burke was in fact much more fond of constraints upon untrammelled power than popular accounts might suggest. He was certainly more sympathetic to American republicans than many late eighteenth-century Canadians were. Other scholars have added that migration across the Canadian-American border meant that many of those who settled in Canada were both familiar with, and sympathetic to, the principles of republican government. There is also the observation that a considerable portion of the population is not (and has never been) an enthusiastic participant in the English Tory tradition.

So what does this mean for the idea of an intellectual tradition in Canadian political thought? Surely political ideas in this country have *some* unifying themes or some coherent direction; they must do more than simply career aimlessly like a drunken cowboy on an empty prairie. Well—yes and no. It is probably unreasonable to expect a relatively young country comprised of countless ethnic groups (at least two of them rather involuntarily) to manifest a clear and unanimous political vision. However, certain motifs do reoccur, and these still play a dominant role in the way in which Canadians view politics. One of these themes is that, for better or for worse, individualism has never become pronounced to the extent that it has in the United States. This theme has manifested itself in a number of ways historically: higher expectations for public order, greater willingness to collectivize public risk, more tolerance (at least recently) for those who have close cultural ties to their community, and so on. But what does this *mean*? The fashionable debate over "identity" has pushed Canada to the forefront of a very vigorous international debate. Canadians, it is said, are more willing than either Americans or most Europeans to tolerate a plurality of identities; this tolerance, many assert, is because of our "Tory" background. Yet this is a curious reading of history. Tories were, in the past, frequently intolerant of any identities beyond their own. In the eighteenth century Americans had a much more vibrant account of tolerance; European and British intolerance was, after all, the reason many had fled to America in the first place.

What made Canada distinct was the *lack* of any real desire to articulate a discrete identity. The purpose of Canada was, in first place, to contain first the French and then the Americans; it was a strategic zone, not a way of life. By the early nineteenth century, it had become clear that discussions of identity were (next to corrupt political opportunism) the most vexatious problem in the colonies. That is why Durham made the horribly unpopular decision to assimilate the French into what he saw as a modern liberal state: he thought that getting *rid* of identities was the only way to move the country forward. Thus the Americans, since their founding, became very much concerned with their identity as *Americans*, while most Canadians over a certain age have never bothered to learn the revised words to their national anthem. Canada, in other words, is a new house left beige so that tenants can decide the colours for themselves. The beigeness of Canada has often been mocked and derided, but, in many ways, Canada's identification with this nondescript hue has made it easier for all kinds of people to live their lives in the colours they choose.

Canadian political identity is thus a dialectic, but this opposition is not simply the conflict between organic Toryism and republican individualism. Certainly, we have the discussion between tradition and modernity and between self and society, and it may well be the case that the contemporary Canadian identity most successfully articulates itself in the tension between these ideas. However, it is important to remember that Canada's success was frequently linked to its ability to downplay identity *per se*. It will be interesting to see how this characteristic fares in an era where Canada is seen as the great experiment in identity theory.

I would like to thank Louise Carbert, Florian Bail, Judy Garber, and Laura Janara, whose intelligent and idiosyncratic insights are really the best part of this job. All those at Broadview have been wonderful to work with. Perhaps all teachers should be given the chance to write the books they wish they had had at their disposal as students; I am grateful to have been given the opportunity to write one of mine. On the domestic frontier, I owe no small amount of gratitude to Gordon, for cutting a swath through the technological jungle for me; to Cheryl, the practically perfect nanny, whose expertise has allowed my mind to stray in comfort from domestic concerns for so many hours a week; and to my children, who never fail to remind me that people—especially little ones—are always more important than ideas.

CHAPTER
1

INTRODUCTION

Can one—ought one—to think about national traits in the development of intellectual thought? Or does the attempt simply reduce a complex heterogeneity of ideas to a set of nationalist clichés? Certainly it is unfair to theorists themselves, as well as to the citizens of any nation, to attribute any inevitability or predictability to their thoughts or values. Nonetheless, few would now admit that complex ideas occur solely through spontaneous generation; there is always an empirical and intellectual background that influences the way in which different groups of people view their world and their time. A more serious objection would be that, while small or homogeneous states might well admit to a clear intellectual trajectory, states with variegated populations inhabiting vast geographical regions may not be as successful.

But it is precisely this lack of a single cultural heritage that has influenced the way in which Canadians view their world. The overwhelming political realities for Canadians involve, as they always have, the question of what to do with groups whose values and understandings are markedly dissimilar. This was Lord Durham's task in 1838: to reorganize the governance of Britain's North American colonies in order to ameliorate the ongoing political conflicts between the French and English. His solution, remarkably modern in many ways, was simply to make the colonists more responsible for their own governance. Less evocative, and considerably more controversial, was his suggestion of a common system of political institutions for a single political entity. For better or for worse, Durham's evaluation of Canadian political relations was the first clear articulation of the issues that would influence the nature of Canadian identity through to the twenty-first century.

Notably, two qualities that were to influence the character of Western liberal states significantly in the twentieth century—democratic governance and the clash of cultures—had been discussed with reference to Canada even before it had become an autonomous political entity. But there is a third dimension to Canadian politics that adds another layer of cultural particularity. "How are we different from Americans?" is a form of parlour game in which all Canadians tend to engage at some point. The broad brushstrokes of our mutual political histories are quite similar: we are both the product of European, largely British, colonial empires; we are staunch defenders of the democratic spirit (however we believe that this ought to be manifest); and we are obliged to accommodate and coordinate citizens with strikingly diverse backgrounds. One contemporary manifestation of this identity game argues that Canadians and Americans have become increasingly divergent in their values. Canadians, according to this account of national identity, have become more tolerant of sexual pluralism and multiculturalism, and they express greater concern for social justice and the environment. Americans fare less well, with a marked rise in consumerism, a greater tolerance of violence, and an untempered nationalism.[1] Other theorists argue that any differences in political values between the two countries are much less significant than the similarities.[2] But why should such divergence exist at all, given the overwhelming similarities between the two states? And, given the modern assumption that globalization consumes all within its gaping maw, why might such divergence be increasing rather than receding?

This is an engrossing question (at least for Canadians!), but this book has no intention of answering it. Rather, it asserts that those who *do* wish to think about such questions should have a good sense of how (and why) Canada's political identity has taken the shape that it has. The objective of this book is modest. It presents no radical reinterpretations of history, nor does it propound any helpful solutions to current political crises. It is merely a pocket roadmap of the intellectual terrain, a brief exegesis of some of the more important political and philosophical debates in Canada's history. It is aimed specifically at those with no extensive or formal training in Canadian political thought; and it will hopefully give them a clearer understanding of why modern political debates in Canada take the form that they do.

For those impatient to become acquainted with contemporary Canadian political thought, the best strategy would be to put down this book and to read Ronald Beiner and Wayne Norman's edited collection *Canadian Political Philosophy*, which offers a broad selection of representative writing from Canada's top contemporary political thinkers.[3] Those who are willing to take a lengthier journey, however, should begin in the eighteenth century. Thus, the purpose of this book is to embark upon a journey, and to arrive at a better understanding of contemporary Canadian political thought through an understanding of how it evolved.

This book, then, is about the development of ideas; and ideas are influenced by both the gritty political realities of the day and the intellectual environment of the time. In more formal words, both empirical and idealist factors are considered to be important causal variables. Somewhat more contentious, perhaps, is the decision to provide a heady mix of proponents of political ideas in a more raw state (generally politicians or activists), political philosophers who offer more refined and critical accounts (such as C.B. Macpherson or Charles Taylor), and those in cognate disciplines (such as history, philosophy, sociology, economics, or literary studies). The point here is not so much to pinpoint an overarching Canadian perspective of political theory as it is to identify relevant clumps of common purpose between those with forceful and coherent ideas. If there is no single school of Canadian political thought, we may at least think of family resemblances between ongoing debates; and, even where heated discussion provides little sense of common purpose, the fact that vociferous debate exists is sufficient evidence that a critical mass of individuals believe an issue important enough to address in no uncertain terms.

But how to select such individuals or ideas? One way is to find ideas that seem to have found resonance with the broader population (such as Tommy Douglas's fight for public health care or Kari Levitt's concern—well before "globalization" was a common term—over American economic influence in Canada). An equally useful method is to determine which ideas provoked the loudest outrage and condemnation; for wherever there is smoke there is fire, and some of the more revered political theorists in Canada are also some of the most reviled. George Grant's *Lament for A Nation* has been beloved by generations of undergraduates, yet George Grant was frequently dismissed as "not a real political philosopher" by many of his peers. Both Pierre Trudeau and René Lévesque, too, were regularly lauded and excoriated by their respective supporters and detractors.

The passage of ideas, then, is frequently confrontational (as Hegel supposed it was), but the variables playing into such a synthesis are vastly greater. This book attempts to address them in a more manageable fashion by looking at distinct sets of themes. The first is the attempt by Canadians throughout their history to distinguish themselves from the two countries that have had the most emphatic influence upon them: the United Kingdom, with its colonial connection to Canada, and the United States, with its strong cultural and economic influences. The second theme looks at the development of a palpable Canadian "social ethos." This, some argue, is a phenomenon that exists primarily in the minds of its exponents. Yet it is true that at least some major policy areas seem to be evidence of a more "progressive" political perspective in Canada. The very existence of a mainstream social democratic party at the national level (as well as the fact that it has formed several governments at the provincial level) adds some heft to this claim. The third theme is the relationship between nations and cultures within Canada, beginning with the struggles surrounding the accommodation of the two dominant cultures and gradually focusing upon the challenges posed by a liberal society containing numerous discrete ethnic groups.

None of these themes is remarkable. Any account probing the nature of Canadian political thought will likely offer up some variation of them. This is a constructive starting point, as it shows that there is, in fact, a great deal of agreement regarding the overarching characteristics of Canadian political thought. When these themes are examined more closely, however, more divergence in opinion arises regarding the formative influence or the particular genesis of specific ideas. How influential was the "Tory tradition" in Canada? What is really meant by a "multicultural" state? Does an emphasis upon the pronounced accommodation of minority cultures enhance or diminish the principles of liberalism in which Canada is grounded? Are Canadians really the proponents of social justice that many would claim, given that several indicators (per capita level of foreign aid, Gini coefficient, child welfare policies) seem clearly to indicate otherwise? And why, given the similarities between Canada and the United States, is there divergence in political values at all?

It is perhaps important to note briefly some of the debates *not* discussed in this book. One theme given short shrift is the debate over the nature of democracy in Canada. The establishment of responsible government in 1848 was the beginning of this discussion, not its culmination; and the discourse over both Confederation and the nature of the new national institutions is certainly worthwhile reading.[4] The second theme is the discussion of federalism as a political institution. Canadians have certainly had a great deal to say about the relationship between federalism and the manifestation of democracy; and their insights have increasingly been applied as a solution to problems of political accommodation throughout the world.[5] A third absent theme looks at the political debates over aboriginal peoples, as well as First Nations' debates with the rest of Canada. Certainly the injustices experienced historically by these groups have been large indeed. The very lack of a clear and sustained political voice for First Nations is itself part of the history of political thought in Canada. This book will not present the historical discussions on record regarding what ought to be done with (or to) aboriginal people in Canada, as aboriginal people themselves were not, until recently, participants in this discussion. Much of the *contemporary* philosophical debate over the place of First Nations is subsumed within the debate over minority rights, which is discussed here. Also, more recently, there have been stimulating debates at a more policy-oriented level on issues regarding First Nations' governance, the accommodation of alienable property rights within a culture of collective ownership, and so on.[6] These debates, as well, are outside the framework of this text.

THE ORGANIZATION OF THIS BOOK

The following chapter looks specifically at the growth and divergence of schools of intellectual thought within the Canadian academy itself. This chapter is designed to be relatively freestanding; one may read it on its own to get a sense of the intellectual context within which ideas developed. Concomitantly, one may skip it altogether and opt for a broader account of the interplay between political ideas and intellectual theories (although the two strands may be frequently difficult to distinguish). One must keep in mind that the wider political culture of a country is not always indicative of its intellectual thought and that the latter is sometimes independent of (and sometimes in opposition to) the former. The provenance of most Canadian political thought in the nineteenth-century was largely in the political arena while, in the late twentieth century, the arguments of academics influenced many fundamental political decisions. On the one hand, mid-nineteenth century debates by politicians over the nature of Confederation provide a rich assortment of complex accounts on the nature of democracy, representation, nationalism, and justice. On the other hand, Canadian universities in the latter half of the twentieth century produced many works of political thought that mirrored the broader distrust of, and opposition to, the conservative outlook of politicians in the earlier half of the century. Canadian nationalism, for example, permeated many, if not most, political science departments in the 1980s, reflecting the broader social trend that culminated in the free trade debates of the latter part of the decade. The recognition of minority rights by the end of the century was also largely a product of academic discourse. One might, of course, object that some of the most formative expression of modern political values has been produced by twentieth-century politicians. A reasonable point: however, it must be tempered with the observation that some of the most galvanizing and influential politicians, such as Lester B. Pearson or Pierre Elliot Trudeau, generally had at least one foot in academia. (Other writers, such as J.S. Woodsworth or Nellie McClung, were, of course, making the point that far too many people were deliberately being denied the opportunity for such systematic intellectual training.)

The third and fourth chapters respectively reflect the concerns first articulated two hundred years earlier: 1) what ought to be Canada's relationship with Britain (and with the United States) and 2) how ought the intractable disputes of "two warring races within the bosom of a single nation" to be resolved? It has been the fate of small countries to be inordinately concerned about their affiliation with more powerful states. Durham's suggestion that Canada ought to be made largely responsible for its own governance was, in retrospect, more the beginning of its troubles than their resolution, as vexatious political issues now had to be addressed by those involved in the disputes rather than by an external authority. What is notable in this trajectory of colony to nation-state is the way in which Canada moulded its vision of responsible government into democratic federalism. Not heeding Durham's advice to formulate a unitary state, the British Crown, in response to vociferous concerns from its colonies, established a number of separate jurisdictions in order to mitigate regional tensions.

Thus, the initial attempts to think about Canada as a single political entity (or the resistance to these attempts) and to consider the shape such a nation ought to take formed the basis of the first substantial body of Canadian political thought. H.D. Forbes, writing in 1984, could casually discuss "the standard pieces" of political theory including "Mgr. Plessis on divine providence, Baldwin on responsible governance, Macdonald on federalism," and so on.[7] However, few political theorists today without a thorough background in Canadian history would be comfortable in referring to these selections as "standard" works. If no longer standard, though, they are certainly important in understanding the genesis of later Canadian thought. What form of "democracy" was appropriate for the new polity? In what way was Canada importantly distinct from Britain? And what important similarities were to be retained? We can easily begin with the latter: Britain's ability to balance a constitutional monarchy with responsible government was, quite rightly, understood as a valuable political legacy. The ideas of "respect for the Throne" and "social order," for example, are most famously evident within the British North America Act of 1867 (later the Canadian Constitution of 1981) in the articulation of "Peace, Order, and Good Government," an idea that has, in turn, affected public policy through its active (and passive) influence upon the development of numerous pieces of legislation.

British Toryism—the belief in the importance of customs, institutions and beliefs that have weathered time and fashion—is thus one important thread in the development of Canadian political thought. From the early Tories of Upper Canada (such as John Strachan, the first Bishop of Toronto) to their more modern manifestations (such as the late Dalton Camp or political columnist Michael Valpy), British values and traditions have been a predominant aspect of Canadianness. And yet this regard for Mother Empire was certainly not universal. Louis-Joseph Papineau bitterly complained in 1833 that

We were told: "You enjoy the English constitution, the freest of any in Europe. Your public bodies are organized in the same fashion as those that have brought Great Britain such greatness and joy." This is an illusion that the majority have taken for reality; a false and lying argument that a few hypocritical partisans have upheld in order to exploit misapprehensions to their profit...."[8]

Like Papineau, Henri Bourassa would later take issue with the obsequiousness and sycophantic behaviour of the Canadian establishment regarding British interests, especially compared, in his view, to the utter disregard shown by Upper Canada to French Canadian interests or sensitivities. And one of the most pressing of these concerns was one shared equally by French and English Canadians: the "spectre of annexation" of the Canadian territories by the United States.

The desire to remain "not American" has, at least for the past two hundred years, continued to be at least as strong a characteristic of Canadian identity as any articulation of British values. Well before waves of postmodern dialogue explained the binary opposition between agent and "Other" (and even before Nietzsche explained how the weak derived a sense of identity in *not* being powerful and oppressive), Canadians have found some comfort in maintaining the distinction between themselves and their closest neighbours. Interestingly, there is little substantive agreement regarding the content of this difference: often the mere *existence* of such differentiation seems more important than the substance of it. What is it about the United States—beyond its rude treatment of Britain in the late eighteenth century—that upsets the Canadian sensibility so frequently? Fear of direct political conquest was replaced some time ago by a more nuanced concern regarding extraterritorial economic control; yet, even in an age of hyperglobalization, the anxiety over creeping Americanism remains. Pollsters, again, point to a recent "value gap" between the two countries; yet the idea of some noxious American culture encroaching upon Canadian values has rather consistently distressed Canadian theorists for a much longer period. George Grant may be the most famous philosophical nationalist of the mid-century, but even Henri Bourassa, hardly known for his Tory sentimentalism, berated his compatriots of Upper Canada on this point in 1912:

American you already are by your language, your nasal accent, your common slang, your dress, your daily habits; by the Yankee literature

with which your homes and clubs are flooded; by your yellow jour-
nals and their rantings; by your loud and intolerant patriotism; by
your worship of gold, snobbery and titles.[9]

It was the French-Canadian fact in Canada, argued Bourassa, that
served as the primary bulwark against cultural absorption into the
United States. (And it was the argument that Canada would never
become a culturally homogeneous nation that led Goldwin Smith
to the opposite conclusion: that Canada must integrate into a continental American state). Bourassa's position is certainly no less
tenable today. "What constitutes Canadian identity, and how can
we reconcile French Canada and English Canada? These questions
are, and have ever been, irreconcilably interwoven—and one could
with just a little irony suggest that the existence of the latter question essentially answers the former.

The fifth and sixth chapters of the book examine the under-
current of social justice that permeates Canadian identity. When
the federal government declared in 2005 that it would significantly
increase disaster relief for South Asia, it announced that this measure was in accordance with "Canadian values." The reference was
understood: it was an implicit characteristic of Canadians to consider
the needs of the less fortunate. Also implicit, yet understood, was
that opposite to those "Canadian values" were the "American values"
of independence and self-reliance. All this occurred at the level of
political rhetoric, but it is significant that no one found this rhetoric particularly remarkable. The concern with equity and social
security, which is frequently articulated as a hallmark of Canadian
identity, is consonant with some empirical data, although it is based
largely upon comparison with the United States and fares less well
when placed within the context of European states. But why does
it exist at all? One explanation that has dominated political theory
was presented by Gad Horowitz, who argued that the political
culture of Canada was largely a reflection of the timing and composition of early immigration patterns. Based upon Louis Hartz's "fragment theory" of political culture, Horowitz's argument is that
Canada contained a "Tory touch" that the United States did not.
Left-wing ideas and values, he suggests, were more likely to develop
in opposition to these Tory principles than to American liberalism,
and this development accounts for the less-individualist nature of

Canadian political culture. Various responses to, and variations of, this "fragment theory" still dominate discussions of Canada's more collectivist and progressive orientation (at least when compared to that of the United States.)[10]

But is this the only explanation? A century ago this concern for the social well-being of others would probably have been viewed as the unremarkable characteristic of a good Christian society. This social concern was especially true of the Methodist church, which was a "highly successful type of religious collectivism" that arose in response to the hierarchical and conservative Anglican Church.[11] "The cultural and moral requirements of Methodism," explains Neil Semple, "demanded the reformation of individuals in the corrupt world. Only by this process could the nation and the world truly progress."[12] The doctrinal expectation placed upon Methodists (and, to a certain extent, upon other evangelical religious groups) to improve the world around them was well suited to the life of pioneers, who faced incredible physical deprivation, cultural alienation, and geographical isolation. By the end of the nineteenth century, the "social gospel" movement encapsulated this belief in man's social responsibility to man, and it laid the foundation for sweeping social reform in the early twentieth century.

Religious ideas have, in this way, had a potent effect upon the existence of a distinct Canadian identity. That theological tenets have an impact upon philosophical ideas, of course, is usually considered fairly self-evident to historians of political thought; it was, after all, particular aspects of Protestant doctrine that allowed for the development of liberal democracy (and, as C.B. Macpherson might contend, for the emergence of capitalism as well). However, in generations conditioned to accept the distinction between politics and religion, where religion is a private matter and political engagement a social responsibility, the causal link between religious doctrine and political values has become obscured. This is not to say that Canadians are particularly devout (compared to contemporary Americans we certainly are not), but, at least in English Canada, our sense of "Canadian identity" can be traced fairly convincingly to the influence of certain Protestant tenets.

The Canadian Left is also very much characterized by its bifurcated history as both an agrarian protest movement (the precursor, ironically, to the modern Reform/Alliance movement) and as a party for urban industrial workers. When one considers the enormous tensions within the evolution of Canadian social democracy, it is rather remarkable that it has survived at all, although, as H.D. Forbes has argued, one unifying feature of the contemporary Canadian Left has been its nationalist focus.[13] As social democratic movements increasingly turn their focus to the issues of global governance, however, it will be interesting to see whether the Left in Canada can remain invigorated without a nationalist focus.

The seventh and eighth chapters of this book examine how the need to accommodate a large French-Canadian population into a workable liberal state required Canadians to think hard very early on about reconciling discrete populations into a larger federal unit. While the political status of aboriginal groups would later be debated with the same intensity as that of French Canada (both groups having been incorporated into English-Canadian culture involuntarily), it was only Quebec that had the political heft, historically, to force this issue on the political agenda at a very early stage. The grand marriage of English and French culture, values, and institutions is perhaps the pre-eminent characteristic of Canada, and the one quality that so early and so easily distinguished Canada from the United States. Given Lord Durham's discussion of Louisiana's place within the United States and his recommendation that Lower Canada ought to have similar status within a united Canada, it is useful to speculate whether such an arrangement would have produced something quite different than the Canada that exists today. Speculation aside, however, the existence of Quebec has provided a distinctive basis for a Canadian identity, even if that identity, at worst, is based upon resentment, suspicion, and fractiousness.

The discussion of Quebec's political thought in this volume focuses exclusively upon Quebec's relationship to the rest of Canada and on its place (for better or for worse) within Canada. Some may object to this emphasis, noting that the intellectual thought of Quebec is vastly more multi-faceted, from its Thomistic schools of philosophy to its interest in continental social thought. Notwithstanding the variegated nature of intellectual writing in Quebec, however, the manifestly *political* thought in the province is still very much dominated by issues of nation, culture, and sovereignty. Those who wish to gain a more profound sense of the richness of Quebec's political thought than that presented here, however, would be well-advised to read Yvan Lamonde and Claude Corbo's *Le rouge et le bleu: une anthologie de la pensée politique au Québec de la Conquête à la Révolution tranquille.*[14]

The impact of Quebec's ongoing discussion regarding culture and political sovereignty has, in the past two decades, had an enormous influence upon both the political aspirations of other cultural groups within (and beyond) Canada and upon the theory of democratic liberalism itself. Here, some argue, Canadian political thought has truly come into its own. For if the logic of cultural sovereignty was at all compelling, then it would surely be relevant to modern aboriginal groups, who had not only the claim of discrete cultural attachment but also of first inhabitation and, in many cases, historical treaties recognizing them as autonomous political units. The limitations of liberal political theory, argue some philosophers, began to be exposed when, over two decades ago, theorists started to ask why, if "universal treatment" was the fundamental principle for liberal values, liberal states took their borders so seriously. If *all* individuals ought to have the right to free movement (or free speech or freedom from cruel and unusual punishment), why did liberal states only protect these rights for their citizens?

I do not think that this question is unanswerable, nor that "sovereign liberal states" must necessarily be contradictions in themselves. But the question was stark enough to catch the intellectual curiosity of a generation of political theorists who saw the paucity of Marxism and the staleness of liberal thought. It also coincided with the intellectual movement of postmodernism, which questioned the strict rationalism or (for some) the stultifying uniformity of liberal principles and which found the subjective questions of identity a welcome relief from the relentless materialism of socialism, welfare liberalism, and libertarianism. The new wave of political thought also fit well with the demographic changes due to immigration in most liberal states, even those that, historically, were based upon a homogeneous ethnic culture. The more "multicultural" and tolerant of difference a state became, went the argument, the more these liberal states were "oppressive" insofar as treating all people the same meant privileging the dominant population.

In sum, this book attempts to identify and to illuminate a number of different threads in the twisted skein of Canadian political thought. In the course of this task, the component parts are isolated and simplified, and critics might argue (rightfully) that the true nature of political thought in Canada is both more complex and more nuanced than the one presented here. But one must begin somewhere. What I have tried to do is to present the ideas as they have influenced intellectual thought in Canada, and I leave it to the readers to judge for themselves the merit of these various discussions. Thus, one might wish to argue that the concept of Toryism is overstated, that George Grant was dangerously wrong-headed, or that minority rights are a step away from justice, rather than toward it (or vice versa). But to critique these accounts, one must first understand them, and understand them within the context within which they were presented. The role of political theory is, quite broadly, to articulate clearly the ideas upon which polities build their social and ethical frameworks; to reflect upon the justifications, and consequences, of these principles; and to assess critically how well these values and institutions serve the people who are subject to them.

The last task, as the final chapter notes, is the most difficult. It is, in the first place, fatuous and uninteresting (as well as unfair) to criticize early theorists using the obvious advantage of hindsight. It is also scoring cheap points to judge early thinkers by their failure to address what are by today's standards clear moral deficiencies in their social values. Temperance? Cultural assimilation? Sterilization for the mentally deficient? Such ideas may well make us shudder delicately today, but they were once part of a web of acceptable beliefs that would have seemed appropriate to any sensible and moral individual a century ago (although, admittedly, the first measure would have had much more widespread opposition than the latter two). In spite of the difficulties inherent in evaluating the political thought of the past, however, we can ask how well ideas have been expressed, or how convincing the justifications, or how incisive the analysis. Relevance is important, but so is vision. Reason and clarity are essential, but why not passion and eloquence? In the end, any critical assessment will rely upon a great deal of subjectivity because any normative rendering of politics will depend upon a particular set of values. Nevertheless, a process of critical evaluation, even when subjective, produces a critical reader (and, hopefully, an engaged citizen). Readers may well not share some of the views underlying the theories presented here, but, hopefully, the book itself will assist them in understanding why they hold the views that they do.

NOTES

1   Michael Adams, *Fire and Ice: The United States, Canada, and the Myth of Converging Values* (Toronto: Penguin Canada, 2003).

2   See, for example, Janet Ajzenstat, *The Once and Future Canadian Democracy: An Essay in Political Thought* (Montreal and Kingston: McGill-Queen's University Press, 2003).

3   Ronald Beiner and Wayne Norman, *Canadian Political Philosophy: Contemporary Reflections* (Don Mills, Ontario: Oxford University Press, 2001).

4   The first, but most inaccessible, set of sources for those interested in pursuing this theme would be the documents (largely letters and speeches) produced by the most influential nineteenth-century politicians (including John A. Macdonald, Charles Tupper, George Brown, George-Étienne Cartier, Thomas D'Arcy McGee, and Wilfrid Laurier). One anthology of these sources is G.P. Brown, *Documents on the Confederation of British North America* (Toronto: McClelland and Stewart, 1969); a more modern one is Janet Ajzenstat, Paul Romney, Ian Gentles, and William D. Gairdner, eds., *Canada's Founding Debates* (1999; Toronto: Stoddart; Toronto: University of Toronto Press, 2003). The second source would be the works of historians writing on this period. Amongst these are Peter Waite, *The Life and Times of Confederation* (Toronto: University of Toronto Press, 1962); Donald Creighton, *The Road to Confederation: The Emergence of Canada, 1863-1867* (Toronto: Macmillan, 1964); W.L. Morton, *The Critical Years: The Union of British North America, 1857-73* (Toronto: McClelland and Stewart, 1964); Ged Martin, *Britain and the Origins of Canadian Confederation, 1937-67* (Vancouver: UBC Press, 1995); and Christopher Moore, *1867: How the Fathers Made a Deal* (Toronto: McClelland and Stewart, 1997). For a more distilled discussion of the nature of democracy within these debates, see Ajzenstat's, *The Once and Future Democracy: An Essay in Political Thought* (previously cited) and Janet Ajzenstat and Peter J. Smith, eds., *Canada's Origins: Liberal, Tory, or Republican?* (Ottawa: Carleton University Press, 1995).

5   See, for example, Herman Bakvis, *Federalism and the Organization of Political Life: Canada in Comparative Perspective* (Kingston: Institute of Intergovernmental Relations, 1981); Jennifer Smith, "Intrastate federalism and confederation," *Political Thought in Canada*, ed. Stephen Brooks (Toronto: Irwin Publishing, 1984) 258-77; Donald Smiley, *The Federal Condition in Canada* (Toronto: McGraw-Hill Ryerson, 1987); R.D. Olling and M.W. Westmacott, eds., *Perspectives on Canadian Federalism* (Scarborough: Prentice-Hall, 1988); Samuel LaSelva, *The Moral Foundations of Canadian Federalism* (Montreal and Kingston: McGill-Queen's University Press, 1996); and Hugh Mellon and Martin Westmacott, eds., *Challenges to Canadian Federalism* (Scarborough: Prentice Hall, 1998).

6   One place to begin is James Frideres, *Aboriginal Peoples in Canada* (Scarborough, ON: Prentice-Hall, 1998). More specific discussions on aboriginal rights and governance can be found in Menno Boldt, *Surviving as Indians: The Challenge of Self-Government* (Toronto: University of Toronto Press, 1993); Alan Cairns, *Citizens Plus: Aboriginal Peoples and the Canadian State* (Vancouver: UBC Press, 2000); Thomas Flanagan, *First Nations? Second Thoughts* (Montreal and Kingston: McGill-Queens University Press, 2000); and Thomas Flanagan and Christopher Alcantana, *Individual Property Rights on Canadian Indian Reserves* (Vancouver: Fraser Institute, 2002). It is also worth reading the *Report of the Royal Commission on Aboriginal Peoples* (Ottawa: Supply and Services, 1998), as well as the numerous support studies published in conjunction with it. One can also find many studies available online from the Institute of Intergovernmental Relations at <http://www.iigr.ca>.

7   H.D. Forbes, ed., *Canadian Political Thought* (Toronto: Oxford University Press, 1985) xi.

8   Quoted in Forbes, *Canadian Political Thought* 18.

9 Henri Bourassa, "The spectre of annexation," 1912, *The Development of Political Thought in Canada: An Anthology*, ed. Katherine Fierlbeck (Peterborough, ON: Broadview Press, 2005) 35.

10 One recent variant of this approach has been published by Grabb and Curtis, who argue that most of Canada and the United States are in fact indistinguishable in their respective value systems and that it is only French Canada (and the American South) that deviate from this "North American consensus." See Edward Grabb and James Curtis, *Regions Apart: The Four Societies of Canada and the United States* (Toronto: Oxford University Press, 2005).

11 Robert F. Wearmouth, *Methodism and the Working Class Movements in England, 1800-1850* (Clifton, NJ: A.M. Kelley, 1972) 224.

12 Neil Semple, *The Lord's Dominion: The History of Canadian Methodism* (Montreal and Kingston: McGill-Queen's University Press, 1996) 66.

13 H.D. Forbes, "Hartz-Horowitz at twenty: nationalism, toryism, and socialism in Canada and the United States," *Canadian Journal of Political Science* 2.20 (June 1987): 287-315.

14 Yvan Lamonde and Claude Corbo, eds., *Le rouge et le bleu: une anthologie de la pensée politique au Québec de la Conquête à la Révolution tranquille* (Montreal: Les Presses de l'Université de Montréal, 1999). For a broader understanding of the development of philosophy in Quebec, consult Yvan Lamonde, *Historiographie de la philosophie au Québec, 1853-1970* (Montreal: Les Cahiers du Québec, 1972); Claude Panaccio and Paul-André Quintin, eds., *Philosophie au Québec* (Montreal: Bellarmin, 1976); and Roland Houde, ed., *Histoire et philosophie au Québec* (Trois-Rivières: Éditions du Bien Publique, 1979).

CHAPTER 2

THE CONTEXT OF
CANADIAN POLITICAL THOUGHT

Is it sufficient merely to recount old theories and past events in order to explain the trajectory of a nation's political thought? No. A purely historical monologue, in addition simply to being tedious, fails to reflect upon why some ideas or values, rather than others, become prominent. Without the question—"why this, and not that?"—any examination of history becomes a dry morsel to choke down. This chapter thus takes a step back from Canadian political thought itself to examine the intellectual context within which it developed; for, to make sense of why political ideas take the shape they have, one must have a clearer understanding of how the phenomenon of politics is studied. The lens provided by the "science of politics" at any given time has had a tremendous influence on the theories produced. For example, the explanation for political behaviour accepted at a particular point will focus upon particular variables (or values) to the exclusion of others, thereby finding only the evidence it was seeking to uncover. If the political claims of workers, or women, or cultural groups, or environmentalists are simply seen as unimportant, then no ambitious academic will focus his energy upon them. If the individual is viewed as the proper unit of society, then the nature of the bonds *between* individuals will probably be neglected. And so on.

It is also difficult to determine whether politics change because of the introduction of new ideas or whether ideas arise in response to a changing political environment (did academics think about Quebec nationalism because it became so important a political phenomenon in the sixties, or did modern Quebec nationalism become so prevalent because academics embraced it?) At the very least, we can say that Canadian political thought is comprised of the interplay between the way in which politics is studied and the political phenomena themselves. Take, for example, the methodological debate over whether academics ought to focus upon institutions and laws or upon the condition of those who had little say in making those institutions and laws. This debate itself politicized radical factions in the sixties by emphasizing the fact that many of the issues most important to the poor and powerless were seen as unimportant by political and intellectual elites.

It is thus important for students of Canadian political thought to have a good sense of their own history *as thinkers*, as well as *as Canadians*. The history of an academic discipline must itself become the subject of investigation because it explains much about how the discipline's own subject matter is understood. Studying a discipline's history is also useful as a reminder of intellectual humility, for we today may simply be blinded by the intellectual fashions of our day and age, just as the behaviouralists or Marxists or postmodernists were limited by theirs.

Although they move more slowly than hemlines, intellectual trends, too, move in accordance with fashion. And, like sartorial trends, intellectual fashions do not stop at countries' borders. To understand why Canadian political thought changed directions when it did, then, one must also consider the wider intellectual context within which it flourished over time. This pattern of intellectual discourse is frequently part of a larger international conversation, and the overarching issues and topics generally tend to be quite similar in most large universities. This tendency becomes especially relevant as communication networks become more sophisticated. To understand how Canadian political theory is distinct from that of any other nation, in other words, one must first see the ways in which it is similar.

With the advantage of a historical perspective, scholars can discern intellectual trends without too much difficulty. All Western states, for example, would have flirted with some variety of Marxism in the late sixties and seventies, although the precise manifestation of Marxist theory would be indicative of the concerns of any particular nation. (Canada, for example, had a particular fascination with dependency theory.) Likewise, the permeation of postmodernism throughout the eighties and nineties was evident in most Western liberal states, although the themes of identity and "différance" had a particular resonance for Canadian intellectuals. The underlying question of this volume is whether it is at all useful to talk in terms of a "Canadian" political theory. Is there, in fact, a way of thinking about politics that is distinctively Canadian? The first section of this chapter takes this discussion a step back and looks at a related question: is there a way of thinking about *thinking* which is distinctively Canadian? This issue has been debated more specifically within the discipline of philosophy, but it has, as we shall see, clear implications for political thought.

Is there such a thing as a "Canadian philosophy"? Speaking at a 1952 symposium on "Philosophy in Canada," Charles Hendel dismissed the existence of a school of philosophy in Canada "which is consciously national in character"; then he deftly declared that "the very immunity of Canadian scholars and philosophers to any such national self-consciousness seems to me their first remarkable characteristic."[1] This quality was, he hastened to add, a manifestation of their maturity, not their innocence of the world. Others have been more willing to identify "Canadian" approaches to the study of philosophy. Not all Americans are pragmatists, not all Germans are idealists, and not all British are analytic, they argue, yet we comfortably speak of the school of "American pragmatism" or "German idealism" or "English analytic philosophy." These national identifications, write Armour and Trott, occur because "philosophy does often grow in response to some need—or, perhaps, the philosophies that attract attention are, not surprisingly, those which are responsive to some felt need."[2]

The link between philosophy itself, then, and the political world that surrounds it is not as disconnected as one might first assume. Yet there has been considerable resistance on the part of many philosophers to any attempt to identify a distinctively Canadian understanding of their reality. These philosophers may simply believe that the proper subject of philosophy must be universal themes, ones not limited by the particular constellation of culture, politics, and geography. But the British empiricism, German idealism, French existentialism, and American pragmatism that developed in response to specific conditions and beliefs were not viewed as being limited to these places; their respective popularity was grounded in the assumption that they transcended specific times and places.

The most developed argument about the nature of Canadian philosophy, a book by Armour and Trott, identifies "philosophical federalism" as the essential Canadian quality of a critical mass of Canadian philosophy. The practice of philosophy in Canada, they argue, was, like much English philosophy of the time, influenced by "philosophical idealism." This simply means that "reality" is independent of thought or, for political theorists, that political events are strongly influenced by ideas (as opposed to, say, material realities, such as the way economic systems are structured). The school of idealism in English Canada was predominantly "post-Hegelian idealism," which focused upon the tension between idealism and community. This, write Armour and Trott, "provided the basis for a logic which, since it saw a dialectical relation between insight and argument, tended to provide a forum within which insights could be assembled."[3] The function of reason, in this account, was less to win arguments and more to accommodate and reconcile differences. But why was this approach so much more pronounced in Canada than, say, in Britain? They suggest that this emphasis occurred because the religious, linguistic, and regional tensions of the country were so obviously relevant to Canadians—tensions between "ideas which made for close-knit organic communities and ideas which demanded plurality and openness."[4]

But even Armour and Trott admit to their critics that this Canadian dimension to philosophy was most pronounced prior to the 1960s, when "philosophers in Canada had been relatively isolated from one another and so had reacted to the general culture and to the other academic interests amongst which they found themselves."[5] After the 1950s, expanding Canadian universities depended more heavily upon "immigrant philosophers," most frequently from the United States, who had little interest in thinking about specifically Canadian concerns. This last point is of particular interest, as it contrasts rather interestingly with political theory, which *began* to develop a nationalist dimension in the 1960s (and has shown very little abatement), even though it faced the same demographic trend of academic immigrants as did the discipline of philosophy.

At a very basic level, the advantage of Canadian political thought over Canadian *philosophy* in the search for a national identity is that the focus of Canadian political thought has generally been upon Canadian politics rather than upon the nature of politics itself. At a more interesting level, however, the same question arises: is there anything distinct or profound about Canadian political thought? Can those with no real interest in Canadian politics find perceptive or universal observations that transcend national boundaries, or is the subject an esoteric field, with limited applicability?

"Political thought," as a field of study, is itself a recent phenomenon (as is the study of political science itself). Prior to the twentieth century, political issues were more properly subsumed within the study of history, classics, and philosophy. If one were interested in the nature of justice, one could study classics (and determine what Plato or Aristotle had to say) or philosophy (and perhaps read Hume or Bentham). If one wished to comprehend how best to govern a fractious polity, those with a philosophical bent could read Machiavelli, while others might simply read historical accounts of how Britain ended up with a constitutional monarchy rather than a bloody revolution. Even the discipline of economics was a branch of philosophy. Adam Smith, a professor of moral philosophy, wrote *The Wealth of Nations* after debating the interrelationship of land, labour, and capital with the French physiocrats. By the late nineteenth century, the rise of economics (both liberal and Marxist) had generated an interest in "political economy": John Stuart Mill published his *Principles of Political Economy* in 1848; Marx's *Capital* came out in 1867. But "political economy" was still philosophy. The study of politics, as we know it today, was based more solidly upon the study of legal institutions, and especially constitutions, which established the foundational principles of a polity. And yet the study of political theory has always had an uncomfortable position within the discipline of political science. In the first place, it focused upon the "soft" normative and ethical issues that many political "scientists," basing their methodology on the disciplines of mathematics, physics, and chemistry, spurned. In the second place, political theory embraced the very methodological debates that inconvenienced those who saw their methodological tools as neutral and objective instruments in their service. However, while political theory often found itself at an arm's length from other forms of political science, it was itself nonetheless influenced by the way in which political science was practiced.

So what, one might ask, *is* "political theory" exactly, and how does it differ from "political science" or "political philosophy"? The short answer is that it depends upon who is using these terms. The slightly more contorted answer is that "political science" *proper* generally refers to the analytical investigation of political phenomenon, with special emphasis upon understanding the causality of political events. "Political philosophy," on the other hand, looks more squarely at the normative or ethical issues involved in the practice of politics (including issues of justice and morality), as well as at the canon of historical thought within which these normative issues were originally framed.

"Political thought" (or political theory) is an odd mongrel, and the term is generally used more loosely than "political philosophy" to refer simply to the ways in which we think about politics and political issues. It can cover the same normative and ethical questions as does political philosophy, although the latter is frequently presented in a more formal and analytical manner. "Political thought" generally accommodates looser discussions of political values, political culture, and methodology, although it should not be taken as a shorthand term for loose thinking. For example, a critical aspect of political theory is its methodological and epistemological dimension: *ought* we, it asks, to approach politics in one way rather than another? In their essay "Where we stand today: the state of modern political science," Theodoulou and O'Brien see their explanation of political science as "the study of political phenomenon [sic] by applying scientific techniques" as a fairly unproblematic definition.[6] A substantial number of political *theorists,* however, would likely be aghast or outraged by this definition, arguing that the very attempt to understand politics "scientifically" rather than, say, historically or "through narrative" itself provides a very selective (and possibly biased) interpretation of political causality.

This brief romp within the discipline of political science, then, is designed to illustrate the wider intellectual culture within which Canadian political theory evolved. But this book is not meant to be a tome about the fusty contours of academic trends (fascinating though they are to some of us fusty academics). Powerful ideas about politics and political values develop in response to a great number of social and cultural forces, and their lack of formal sophistication is no reflection on their salience or depth. Nellie McClung's chatty and entertaining essays on the condition of women in Canada at the beginning of the twentieth century, for example, are no less penetrating in their understanding of the social dynamics of gender for their lack of formal academic presentation:

"Who will mind the baby?" cried one of our public men, in great
agony of spirit, "when the mother goes to vote?" One woman replied
that she thought she could get the person that minded it when she
went to pay her taxes....7

Irony and wit are also potent ways of presenting a point, and, through
this passionate and often entertaining exposition of issues, individuals with burning ideas were able to force these ideas on the intellectual agenda. At the beginning of the twentieth century, however,
the study of politics was predominantly the study of formal legal
institutions, and political theory, at best, concerned itself with the
values that legal documents (such as constitutions) ought to embody.

THE INSTITUTIONAL (FORMAL-LEGAL) APPROACH

As Bernard Crick famously noted, the history of political science is
the history of American political science.[8] While political science as
a discipline existed in the United States in the latter part of the nineteenth century, the American Political Science Association was not
formalized as a professional association until 1903. What distinguished political science as a discipline from this point up to World
War II was its focus on the formal legal institutions of political life
and, particularly, on the constitutions and other legal frameworks
upon which governing institutions were based. What powers ought
the executive to have? What was the proper balance between legislative and judicial bodies? This focus on the nature of political institutions was not surprising; the political history of the United States
was grounded upon the consideration of how best to design political institutions in order to avoid the worst excesses of European
monarchical systems. Those who framed the American constitution
had a sound comprehension of modern political theory: their
concern with a "balance of power" in government is a clear echo of
the French theorist Montesquieu's study of (rather ironically) English
constitutional monarchy, while a large number of rights and liberties articulated by the American constitution reflect John Locke's
criticism of Britain's failings in maintaining a system of justice for
its citizens.[9] Moreover, as Baxter-Moore, Carroll, and Church explain,
most early practitioners of political science were trained as legal

scholars in areas such as jurisprudence or constitution law. And, as they also note, "the nineteenth century was the age of constitution making in Europe and North America, as new and old states alike sought to adjust to the political and social upheaval of the industrial revolution."[10]

THE "SCIENCE" OF POLITICS: POSITIVISM, BEHAVIOURALISM, AND SYSTEMS THEORY

The landscape of political science changed dramatically with World War II. There are at least three reasons for this. In the first place, the study of institutions and constitutions alone could not give a profound explanation for why fascism had developed so emphatically in Europe; Germany's Weimar Republic, after all, was formally a model of good liberal constitutionalism. In the second place, the anti-Semitic measures increasingly prevalent in Germany prior to World War II led to a vast exodus of German Jewish academics. Many of these had been strongly influenced by the "Vienna School" of logical positivism, which stressed a more scientific, empirical approach to knowledge. The vapid liberalism characterizing the political science of the day, these exiles argued, was insufficient to grasp what was really occurring in the political domain. Bringing their views and their training to bear on the discipline, these individuals were instrumental in developing the behaviouralist movement in Britain and North America. Rather than focusing upon institutions, this approach investigated the behaviour of individuals in a given context. Crucial to this approach was the methodology required in arriving at conclusions. Speculative, historical, and narrative approaches were spurned in favour of an objective "scientific" methodology that stressed observation and verification. The third reason for the growth of behaviouralism stems from the second. By the early 1950s, the economic growth of the United States had become a remarkable phenomenon, and the business of creating consumer goods and selling them was addressed with scientific precision. Advertising firms and marketing agencies began to realize how useful the tools of social science could be in determining potential consumers, and quantitative research methodology became increasingly more sophisticated as its potential for making profits was realized.

By the early 1960s, the assumption that the study of politics ought to be grounded upon a scientific methodology was quite dominant, and the legacy of this era (which also coincided with the expansion of universities) can be found in the designation of "Political *Science*" for so many of these new departments. The focus on scientific methodology at this time had at least two distinct manifestations. The empiricists, who were strongly influenced by behaviouralists in the scientific disciplines (such as B.F. Skinner), argued that investigators ought to concern themselves only with observable and measurable data, which could be noted and recorded in a clear and objective manner. While behaviouralists examined tangible raw data and extrapolated their theories from it, systems theorists did the opposite by looking at the complex relationships between numerous interrelated orders. Accounts such as the "systems analysis" approach of David Easton and the "structural functionalist" approach of Gabriel Almond stressed the primacy of specific economic and social variables (such as voting behaviour) in explaining political outcomes. Thus behaviouralists began their research from the bottom and built their theories "up," while systems analysts favoured a "top-down" methodology that focused upon a holistic analysis of many divergent systems. Both schools of thought, however, were clearly influenced by scientific methodology, and both were instrumental in divorcing the study of politics from history and classics, which remained in the fuzzier "humanistic" disciplines. The emphasis upon data gathering and complex statistical analysis, along with the development of computer technology that can accommodate massive data inflow and processing, remains a hallmark of "American" political science.

RADICAL APPROACHES

By the late 1960s, new generations of scholars began to argue that an obsession with quantification meant that vital aspects of political life were being neglected. Scientific methodology meant that a deeper understanding of why certain phenomena occurred was possible, but it did not permit an incisive examination of whether these developments were positive ones or not. Value decisions, in other words, were devalued within the discipline. But normative concerns began to be more pronounced both within the discipline and within society more widely: and traditional political science was increasingly seen as innately conservative, at best, and as a systematic defender of the status quo, at worst.

As the political threats posed by the Cold War began to recede, Americans became more aware of the problems within their own society. The Vietnam War protests were the most evident of these, but issues of race and gender became articulated with greater resentment, as did a recognition of urban and regional poverty. Marxist theory became quite prevalent in political science studies during this time; it was, argued many, relevant academically because it offered both an analytical approach to understanding power as well as a normative critique of the power holders that was neglected in behaviouralist approaches. The Marxist theory of this time had very much an American stamp, for, while the late 1960s and 1970s was fertile ground for the exposition of left-wing ideas, Marxism had been quite influential for a group of American theorists for several decades.

This group of scholars, known as the Frankfurt School, was also largely comprised of Jewish exiles from Germany, but their approach was considerably different than that of the logical positivists. Founded initially to study the works of Marx, members of the Frankfurt School developed interests in Freudian theory, social philosophy, and modern culture. Their focus remained the study of oppression and liberation in contemporary society, but because the dynamics of class and discussions of economic domination were more oblique in their works, the "radical" approach of the Frankfurt School was much more palatable to Americans, who remained highly uneasy of any favourable references to communism. Their ideas were not a dominant influence in American political science during the 1940s and 1950s, but they rebounded in popularity in 1960s largely due to the School's affiliation with Eric Fromm and Herbert Marcuse. Marcuse, especially, was able to present accessible accounts of psychological and political alienation, which found resonance with undergraduates in the 1960s and 1970s.

The Left in the United States was not as successful in capitalizing upon the resurgence of radical politics as were other dispossessed groups.[11] Even Marcuse eventually saw the Left's redemption in the United States as dependent upon the Black Power or Women's Liberation movements. In a sense, he was correct; it was largely the development of feminism and feminist epistemology that ultimately and effectively challenged the claim of scientific methodology to be the only effective methodology in the social sciences.

THE STRAUSSIANS

The Straussians comprise yet another school whose origins can be traced to Jewish exiles. They are a small but provocative group of political theorists who follow the ideas outlined by Leo Strauss. While he declared his interest to be simply the study of the history of political thought, Strauss's interpretations of Plato and others are often viewed by non-Straussians, writes Neil Robertson, "as idiocratic, perverse, or simply bizarre."[12] Indeed, as Robertson suggests, it is more useful to see Strauss (and his followers) as critics of contemporary political thought than as mere interpreters.

The Straussians' concern is that of "the crisis of the West," with its emphasis upon self-interest over virtue and individual rights over the collective good. Yet it is not their subject matter but their methodology that receives the most attention. The fate of Socrates, they hold, is a lesson for all real philosophers, for the Truth is dangerous and cannot be widely spoken. Political philosophers must therefore be cautious how they write; their ideas must be passed to disciples through code. Only by mastering the "esoteric art of writing" can one gain the keys to interpreting the ahistorical message that great political philosophers have attempted to keep alive, but out of the dangerous hands of the unenlightened masses.

Despite being viewed by mainstream political theorists as a rather eccentric academic cult, Straussians have generally gained a reputation as having a solid knowledge of historical texts, and their criticism of modernity is frequently not too removed from that of the conservative portion of the American population. Indeed, Shadia Drury argues that Straussians in the United States have had a disproportionate influence upon key political figures in the recent Republican administrations.[13]

RATIONAL CHOICE THEORY

Despite the challenges posed by critics of classic behaviouralism, quantitative methodology has continued to figure prominently in American political science. Robert Dahl famously argued that the increasingly lower profile of behaviouralism was in fact evidence of its success, as it showed that the principles of behaviouralism had been incorporated into most mainstream political science. In a sense, he was correct: modern political science is to a large extent "an attempt to improve our understanding of politics by seeking to explain the empirical aspects of political life by means of methods, theories, and criteria of proof that are acceptable according to the canon, conventions, and assumptions of modern empirical science."[14] While radical theories had a significant impact upon political science from the late 1960s, they were never able to form a hegemonic dominance over mainstream political science, which had been largely constructed on the principles of behaviouralism. By the end of the 1980s, political science clearly had bifurcated into two predominant streams: radical approaches became less interested in Marxist ideas but more captivated by continental social theory (including feminist analysis, hermeneutics, psychoanalysis, and postcolonialism, amongst other schools) while the orthodoxy became influenced by developments within the discipline of economics. By 1992, Theodore Lowi was directing his Presidential Address to the American Political Science Association to the investigation of "why public choice has become probably the hottest thing going in political science today."[15]

Rational choice (or public choice) theory is an abstract model that focuses directly upon individual decision making. Directly refuting assumptions of both classical pluralism and orthodox Marxism, rational choice theory holds that individuals are naturally self-interested and that the sum of rational individual actions may well be collectively irrational. Early examples of this approach are Anthony Downs's *An Economic Theory of Democracy* (1957) and Mancur Olson's *The Logic of Collective Action* (1965). Later accounts focused more upon the principles of game theory. The attraction of this approach rests, to a certain extent, in the concern felt by many political scientists of the early 1970s that both the Left and the mainstream orthodoxy had placed too much emphasis upon "social forces" or "systems," leaving little room for individual volition as an explanatory variable. Somewhat ironically, the overwhelming popularity of rational choice theory led others to complain later that political explanation now focused too narrowly upon the choices made by individuals and neglected the way in which individuals were, in turn, influenced by their "context of choice." It would seem that this methodological deficiency could be remedied by making an effort to understand why, beyond mere "self interest," individuals make the decisions they do. Yet rational choice theorists proved to be quite resistant to examining the complex motivations of individual decision makers because, as they argued, doing so would involve a great deal of non-quantifiable (or not easily quantifiable) information. Others, such as Lowi, suggest that the "objective" nature of rational choice theory hides an implicit normative orientation that is indisputably conservative. For example, rational choice theory is by its very nature an economic approach, and so an emphasis upon rational choice theory in public policy-making means that economics becomes "the language of the state." But, as Lowi argues, "economic analysis is so useful because it closes off debate": only issues that can be measured, quantified, and subjected to formulae (such as balanced budgets) are kept on the political agenda. Messy, unquantifiable, and value-laden issues (such as the importance of cultural integrity for minorities) are allowed to slide off of it.

POSTMODERNISM

By the end of the 1980s, Marxist theory reached its nadir. The demise of the largest communist state, the Soviet Union, seemed to many to be evidence of the obvious superiority of liberal democracy, and issues of gender and culture, which were given less importance in Marxist theory, seemed increasingly relevant. Radical academics, who took a less sanguine view of the merits of liberalism, began to focus upon the theories of "postmodernity" coming from continental Europe.

The philosophical tradition of "anti-liberal" thought has arguably existed for as long as liberal thought. During the eighteenth century, Hume and Rousseau had, in their own ways, questioned the role of rationalism in politics, and the Romantic theorists of the early nineteenth century systematically challenged rationalism, universalism, and humanism as political foundations, stressing instead qualities such as imagination, creativity, and passion. Perhaps the most articulate "anti-liberal" political theorist was Friedrich Nietzsche, who contested both the liberal democratic assumptions of modern states and the scientific basis of knowledge that underpinned them.

But contemporary postmodernism was perhaps rooted more firmly in the existentialism of twentieth-century Europe, especially after the wave of fascism receded to expose the horrific consequences of putatively "modern" social policy. While many themes of existentialism itself can be traced to Nietzsche or Kierkegaard, the twentieth century brought with it the overwhelmingly dominant forces of capitalism and consumerism, and theorists were able to contrast the spiritual deprivation of modern man with the considerable excesses of technological progress. Far from realizing their oppression in the diminution of their creative potential, however, postwar generations seemed to revel in the bloated consumerism and moral permissiveness of the late twentieth century even as the costs of untrammelled liberalism became increasingly apparent.

But the social sciences at this point were locked in a deep embrace with quantitative methodologies, so the task of critiquing the underlying assumptions of this approach fell largely to the humanities. Literary theory and, to a lesser extent, philosophy became a bulwark for postmodernism at this early stage, and the tendency of many disciplines to rely upon a heavily structured understanding of function and causality led to an intellectual movement toward "post-structuralism." Thus, Jacques Derrida focused upon the flux of "discourse" in comprehending ideas, in contrast to the belief that meaning was fixed, and Michel Foucault argued that the nature of power in society was diffuse, opaque, and multidirectional rather than a rigid force centred solely within the formal institutions of a state. Jean-François Lyotard famously stated the need for a "scepticism of metanarrative" or a repudiation of the belief that there exists one overarching truth.

It is easy to see why these ideas became increasingly appealing to disenchanted radicals. The rigid and formulaic nature of much of contemporary Marxism was increasingly rejected as a basis for understanding the lot of the oppressed and dispossessed, and, throughout the 1990s, postmodernism became a dominant alternative to heavily quantitatively oriented political science. At an epistemological level, the radical scepticism of the postmodernists challenged the values upon which "objective" political science was based as well as the interests that it served. Feminists, while preceding the wave of postmodernism, nonetheless found many of its ideas (such as the nature of power) useful in their analyses, as did those with an interest in race relations or "postcolonialism."

Nonetheless, the initial enthusiasm for postmodernism became dampened by the extraordinarily dense and difficult style of writing employed by many postmodernists. Defenders argued that there was a sound basis for the rarefied jargon and convoluted sentences: readers were expected to create their own particular meaning out of what they read— clarity was, by definition, oppressive. However, renouncing the possibility of a writer clearly conveying thought also meant that much uncritical drivel was published, a fact brought home by the "Sokal hoax," where a sceptical professor of physics published a deliberately nonsensical article, written in high postmodern style, in a well-regarded journal.[16]

The stridency of postmodernism in political science became much more muted by the turn of the millennium. Its obvious epistemological weaknesses were matched by the downside of its emphasis upon moral relativism: while most proponents of postmodernism tended to be concerned with the plight of the less fortunate, the moral relativity of postmodernism prevented them from critiquing those who were patently apathetic to such ends (or even cheerfully in favour of dominance and oppression). This consequence Nietzsche himself had pointed out a century before. The very ideas that made postmodernism appealing and distinctive, then, also restricted its ability to defeat other methodological approaches. As with behaviouralism, however, the triumph of postmodernism has been in its ability to infiltrate the "orthodoxy" with ideas, once radical, that are now taken largely for granted. The limits of rationality are now acknowledged, even as the tools of science are regularly employed; the claim that power is a diffuse rather than unidirectional force is seen as unproblematic; and few contemporary individuals are unreservedly positive about the forces of modernity.

NEO-ROMANTICISM

The current period of political science, argue the optimists, marries the best of traditional scientific methodology with the sceptical insights of postmodernity. This "new eclecticism" recognizes that "there is an explicit place for normative considerations alongside empirical applications in the study of politics."[17] The more pessimistic, however, will wander through the massive American political science conferences, where enclaves of rational choice theorists or postmodernists discuss their findings, and will note that the existence of these enclaves does not mean that the proponents of either actually wish to engage in conversation with the other. The "new eclecticism" may, according to the pessimists, be more of a "new polarization," with the sheer volume of political scientists in the United States alone permitting the existence of discrete and complex debates within, though not between, both camps.

It should be noted that the intellectual polarization evident in the United States is (like many things) much more muted in Canada. The trajectory of Canadian political science was initially slightly different from that of the United States because, unsurprisingly, of its intellectual ties with Great Britain. Political scientists were more likely to be trained at Oxbridge or in London rather than in the United States, where institutional approaches were becoming increasingly influenced by the Chicago School of Economics (which later developed into the behaviouralist movement). At the University of Toronto, for example, politics was clearly subsumed within political economy, in keeping with the British tradition. The most prominent political scientist of the prewar period was Harold Innis, whose work has been described as a materialist approach without a class analysis. (Interestingly, however, Innis's own intellectual influences were predominantly American, from his graduate training in Chicago to the impact on his thinking of F.J. Turner's "frontier thesis," which stressed the influence of American geography on its society and politics.)

After World War II, the economic focus of Canadian political thought began to be displaced by interest in the formal institutional studies that had characterized American political science some decades earlier. Part of the reason for this shift was the rapid development of federal-provincial dynamics brought about by the growing political maturity of the provinces. Another part of the explanation, as Baxter-Moore, Carroll, and Church note, was the "relative underdevelopment" of the rich descriptive studies needed to understand more fully how the Canadian political system worked.[18] However, the major impact of American political science upon Canada occurred in the 1960s and 1970s, when the growth of political science departments could not keep up with the number of Canadians being trained as political scientists. Few departments during the 1970s were not characterized by a large coterie of American scholars, and with the immigration of American intellectuals came the importation to the discipline of various forms of behaviouralism and systems analysis.

One must keep in mind that scientific methodology was not the only intellectual influence on Canadian political science. Straussianism was another. And the need to import American academics also coincided with the desire of some American scholars to avoid being drafted to serve in the Vietnam War, so a certain percentage of American political scientists also happened to bring radical intellectual ideas with them. But the radicalism of the United States had focused upon race, inner city poverty, and Vietnam, none of which were burning issues in Canada at the time. What *was* relevant to Canadians (and to Canadian academics) was the United States itself—and the influence it had upon Canadian society.

In 1970, Kari Levitt published her seminal study of American branch plants in Canada, which argued that increasing levels of American ownership in the Canadian economy had a direct impact upon the ability of the country to govern itself autonomously. Levitt's study was based upon a stream of Marxist theory (articulated especially well by André Gunder Frank), which argued that poverty (particularly in Latin America) was a direct consequence of American capitalist expansion. Throughout the 1970s and 1980s, the school of "new Canadian political economy" evolved, which used a Marxist framework but focused particularly upon the political consequences of American capital in Canadian business. References were made to Innis's focus upon "staples" or natural resources as a determinant of broader social and political phenomena in Canada. The political economy approach both reflected the mood of anti-Americanism and contributed to it. It was, in a self-referential way, the identification of a nascent international concern for the effects of globalization. The debate over the role of American capital culminated in the discussions of whether to embark upon a policy of freer trade with the United States. Canadian nationalism was a fierce public sentiment, but more prosaic studies (such as the 1985 Macdonald Commission report on "the state of the economic union") argued that such noble passions would likely result in declining economic indicators.

By the 1990s, interest in Canadian nationalism became increasingly eclipsed by the study of nations *within* Canada. This trend was not in itself autochthonous; American politics had similar discussions about political apathy and the communitarian alternatives to liberal thought. What the United States did not have, however, was the threat of succession by a large, culturally distinct political entity. The concept of nationalism based explicitly upon cultural distinctiveness has had a long and relatively unbroken history within Quebec, although what was particularly effective about the nationalism of the Quiet Revolution was, first, the attempt to separate political and cultural sovereignty from religious concerns and, second, the clear analysis of the way in which cultural domination resulted in systematic economic hardship. The idea of culturally specific sovereignty was cemented into the national consciousness by the establishment of political parties in Quebec whose very raison d'être was to oversee the transition to sovereignty, as well as by the Quebec referenda of 1980 and 1995, which showed Canadians that the political will for independence was quite resolute. Aboriginal groups, too, became more politically active in the 1990s; the political standoff at Oka in 1990 between the Mohawks from the Kanesatake reserve and the Canadian Forces was only the most publicly visible of a number of confrontations between aboriginal groups and government agencies.

The emergence of "minority rights" as a focus for political theory thus had its roots in a number of different trends. The most immediate, as noted above, was the growing political consciousness of culturally discrete groups. Throughout most of Canada's history, the English heritage of the country was unapologetically dominant. The values of Englishmen were viewed (especially by the English political elites) as obviously superior and thus desirable; all other cultural values and practices were devalued, at best, or obliterated, at worst. Immigrant groups, like the aboriginal peoples, both absorbed and resented these values. Yet by the 1970s, liberal cosmopolitanism had become fashionable and "ethnicity," as long as it remained within clearly circumscribed boundaries, was celebrated. By the 1990s, however, this "food, clothing, and dance" multiculturalism was being challenged by a more fundamental modulation in thinking.

Intellectual shifts, too, were intersecting with these social changes. The broad impact of postmodernism was significant, both in its challenge to the idea that "liberal" values were necessarily neutral and value-free and in its exhortation to give non-dominant voices respect and consideration. However, not all intellectual figures were working explicitly within this paradigm. Charles Taylor's study of Hegelian thought, for example, was to become quite influential in the challenge to liberal individualism. Influenced strongly by the German Romantic movement, which was itself a challenge to the principles articulated by Enlightenment philosophers, Hegel endeavoured to reconcile the Enlightenment principles of reason and logic with the Romantic emphasis upon freedom and creativity. Hegel found his synthesis in the attempt to understand a fully realized individual as someone who could only develop within the context of his community and in the assertion that freedom and creativity are most fully attained in an ordered, structured environment. But another aspect of German Romanticism, again in response to Enlightenment rationalism, emphasized the way in which individuals exist and find meaning within a context of language and culture that cannot be reduced to the dictates of reason. Both Johann Gottfried von Herder and August Wilhelm Schlegel, the first writing at the end of the eighteenth century and the second at the beginning of the nineteenth, investigated the importance of language and folk traditions not only to "the soul of the race" but also (in good Romantic fashion) to the formation of an *individual's* sense of his own self.

Yet these ideas remained relatively abstruse and politically irrelevant in Canada until the publication of Will Kymlicka's *Liberalism, Community, and Culture* in 1989, which made these ideas accessible and pertinent. Kymlicka posed the central issue quite clearly: traditional liberal rights were simply not meaningful to individuals in some cultural groups because they did not protect what was most important to them. Traditional cultural values and practices were being undermined by the sheer dominance of mainstream western culture, yet orthodox liberal theory determined that, because the political rights of individuals in these cultural groups were not threatened, no state remedy was required. Cultural qualities, unlike political rights or even material well-being, fall within the realm of the personal, not the public, and therefore ought, according to liberal principles, to be left to the individual (or to the marketplace). However, objects Kymlicka, if one's cultural practices and beliefs are integral to one's individuality, then does not the dissolution of one's culture also mean the destruction of the individual within that culture? Further, if we profess to be good liberals, should we not concern ourselves with the well-being of fellow citizens as *individuals?* If protecting individuals within imperilled cultures means strengthening and supporting the cultural group itself, then it follows that the establishment of minority group rights under certain conditions is the proper responsibility of a liberal state.

Kymlicka's book, and the works that followed, changed the contours of political thought in Canada in an explosive way, and the discussion of minority rights has since dominated Canadian political thought. Charles Taylor's book, *The Malaise of Modernity* (published, interestingly, as *The Ethics of Authenticity* in the United States), proved to be equally accessible. It, like his more academic work *The Sources of the Self,* described how liberalism has increasingly impoverished the individual by focusing upon a particularly flat conception of selfhood. James Tully, too, has written of the need to protect a "cultural individualism" in an increasingly pluralistic society.[19]

What these and many other current works of Canadian political thought have in common is a challenge to the atomism in political thought that remains a significant legacy of the Enlightenment. The emotional and psychological well-being of individuals is considered to be at least as important (if not more important) than their freedom from state sanction; and (like many German Romantics) the focus of individual well-being in this approach is understood within the context of cultural rootedness. The very success of liberalism now defines its weaknesses, as the provision of political freedoms and some degree of material well-being now compel us to examine more closely the *humanity* of these living ciphers. Scientific rationalism cannot tell us much about the passions and desires of the human spirit, argued the Romantic philosophers; therefore, how can we comprehend what it truly means to be a human without understanding how these qualities manifest themselves? The focus for modern political theory is thus not simply on what is necessary to recognize individuals as equal political units, but also on what makes life *meaningful* for them.

The answer frequently given is similar to that proposed by the Romantics: what makes life meaningful for us is our relationship to other individuals. And this relationship is not merely about the physical capacity of some to prevent others from (or compel them to) certain kinds of actions that they find abhorrent or uncomfortable. It is also about the way in which they are made to feel anguish or joy, embarrassment or pride, alienation or security. Unlike the communitarian trend that was apparent during the 1980s and early 1990s, however, the current focus defines the relevance of the group with reference to the needs of the individual, rather than the contrary. This is why the latest turn in political theory seems to have a "neo-romantic" quality to it.

Janet Ajzenstat has argued that, rather than understanding Canadian political thought as a continuum of conservative, liberal, and socialist thinking, we should view it as a (rather acrimonious) debate between liberals and Romantics.[20] Cavillers may complain that this tells us little: there are few concepts more vague and amorphous than "liberalism," they might argue, but "romanticism" is certainly one of them. Yet Ajzenstat is undoubtedly correct in pinpointing the locus of disagreement between traditional liberals, who support the value of undifferentiated political equality and who believe in the capacity of a state to do so in a relatively neutral way, and those who argue that the practice of equal treatment among unequals merely emphasizes and entrenches such inequality.

One would do well not to overstate the neo-romanticism of recent political thought. Very few theorists who stress the group orientation of individual life wish to jettison completely many of the liberal values and institutions that remain the hallmark of a civil, and civilized, society (including transparency, due process, and numerous human rights). The effort, at best, is rather to reconcile the two streams—community and individuality—in order to find the best of both worlds. This endeavour is not particularly new; Hegel made it his life's project. Yet other theorists are rather concerned that this new focus on the subjectivity of everyday life may act as a smokescreen behind which nefarious acts are committed against vulnerable peoples. Politically, the fault line for this new debate, both locally and internationally, is between the unity of a cohesive, functional society and the nurturing of individuals' sense of identity and selfhood. And this dialectic is unrepentantly woven into the tissue of Canadian life. As Northrop Frye wrote in 1971, "when the CBC is instructed by Parliament to do what it can to promote Canadian unity and identity, it is not always realized that unity and identity are quite different things to be promoting."[21] The tension, in other words, does not simply underlie Canadian politics; it also defines it.

NOTES

[1] Charles Hendel, "The character of philosophy in Canada," *Philosophy in Canada: A Symposium*, ed. John Irving (Toronto: University of Toronto Press, 1952) 27.

[2] Leslie Armour and Elizabeth Trott, *The Faces of Reason: An Essay on Philosophy and Culture in English Canada, 1850–1950* (Waterloo: Wilfrid Laurier Press, 1981) 15.

[3] Elizabeth Trott and Leslie Armour, "*The Faces of Reason* and its critics," *Dialogue* 25 (1986): 111.

[4] Leslie Armour, "Canadian philosophy: the nature and history of a discipline? A reply to Mr. Mathien," *Dialogue* 25 (1986): 75.

[5] Armour, "Canadian philosophy" 77.

[6] Stella Theodoulou and Rory O'Brien, "Where we stand today: the state of modern political science," *Methods for Political Inquiry: The Discipline, Philosophy, and Analysis of Politics*, eds. Stella Theodoulou and Rory O'Brien (New Jersey: Prentice Hall, 1999) 1.

[7] Nellie McClung, "Hardy perennials," 1915, *The Development of Political Thought in Canada: An Anthology*, ed. Katherine Fierlbeck (Peterborough, ON: Broadview Press, 2005) 48–49.

[8] Bernard Crick, *The American Science of Politics: Its Origins and Conditions* (London: Routledge and Kegan Paul, 1959).

[9] See, for example, Annabel Patterson's discussion of Locke in *Early Modern Liberalism* (Cambridge: Cambridge University Press, 1997).

[10] Nicolas Baxter-Moore, Terrance Carroll, and Roderick Church, *Studying Politics* (Toronto: Copp Clark Longman, 1994) 6.

[11] See Richard Rorty, *Achieving Our Country: Leftist Thought in Twentieth-Century America* (Cambridge, MA: Harvard University Press, 1998).

[12] See Neil Robertson, "Leo Strauss's Platonism," *Animus: A Philosophical Journal for our Time* 4 (1999), 13 Sept. 2005 <http://www.swgc.mun.ca/animus/1999vol4/roberts4.htm>.

[13] For further information on Strauss and Straussians, see Shadia Drury, *The Political Ideas of Leo Strauss* (New York: St Martin's Press, 1988) and *Leo Strauss and the American Right* (New York: St Martin's Press, 1997).

[14] Robert Dahl, "The behavioralist approach in political science: epitaph for a monument to a successful protest," *The American Political Science Review* 55.4 (December 1961): 763-72.

[15] Theodore Lowi, "The state in political science: how we become what we study," *American Political Science Review* 86.1 (March 1992): 1-7.

[16] See Alan Sokal, "Transgressing the boundaries: towards a transformative hermeneutics of quantum gravity," *Social Text* (Spring/Summer 1996): 217–52.

[17] Theodoulou and O'Brien, "Where we stand today" 9.

[18] Baxter-Moore et al, *Studying* 15. See also C.B. Macpherson, "After strange goods: Canadian political science in 1973," *Perspectives on the Social Sciences in Canada*, eds. T.N. Guinsburg and G.L. Reuber (Toronto: University of Toronto Press, 1974) 52–76.

[19] James Tully, *Strange Multiplicity: Constitutionalism in an Age of Diversity* (Cambridge: Cambridge University Press, 1995).

[20] Janet Ajzenstat, *The Once and Future Democracy: An Essay in Political Thought* (Montreal and Kingston: McGill-Queen's University Press, 2003).

[21] Northrop Frye, preface, *The Bush Garden: Essays on the Canadian Imagination* (Toronto: Anansi Press, 1971) ii.

PART
1

NATION

3 THE COLONIAL LEGACY

The British colonial legacy in Canada is both powerful and contradictory. One aspect of this intellectual heritage, Toryism, is itself hardly a coherent idea. The term, from the Irish *tóraidhe* (outlaw), was originally used as a derisive epithet in the seventeenth century, and, by the eighteenth century, it was the marker for those who supported the rights and privileges of the Crown in opposition to those who favoured expanding the powers of Parliament. In pre-Confederation Canada, the term was used loosely to denote those who supported the monarchy (and thus British rule of Canada) in contrast to those who sympathized with the principles of American republicanism. Later, prominent central Canadian business elites became labelled "Blue Tories," while those who held conservative beliefs but chafed under the political and economic control of central Canada became known as "Red Tories." When the Conservative party began to attract proponents of limited government, individual rights, and freer trade (also referred to, confusingly, as "classical liberals"), the term "Red Tory" became what "Tory" itself had originally meant: the belief that the common good was more important than individual right, that a set of traditional (generally Christian) values were the proper foundation of moral life, and that traditional customs and beliefs were superior to rationalist principles as a basis for social and political institutions.

The second intellectual stream that influenced Canadian political thought is the tradition of British liberalism and constitutionalism. This stream is derived from the British "Whig" tradition, which stressed constitutionalism as a limit to arbitrary monarchical power. The two traditions are neither clearly complementary nor mutually exclusive, and the reader may well be forgiven some confusion. Burke's defence of English traditionalism against French revolutionary activity was a response to the increasing acceptance of the doctrine of natural rights, the idea that individuals simply had rights in their capacity as individuals that were prior to and superior to any claims a society had upon them. In this, he was obviously a conservative. But what he was trying to conserve were the concessions granted to Englishmen in 1689. These political rights are generally subsumed under the formal institutional label of "constitutional monarchy," which, simply put, is the stipulation that the Crown must observe certain restrictions upon its power. Thus, British constitutionalism is in fact ingrained in the Tory tradition, yet its political counterpoint—American republicanism—is as well.

This chapter and the next will treat each strand of thought as if it were a discrete and consistent line of thinking. This is done solely for the purpose of clarity in description. But keep in mind that ideas are not bugs to be netted and pinned, legs counted, onto boards. The process of labelling and categorizing historical ideas is far more difficult and contentious than the following narrative suggests. Whether one person's thought is seen as conservative, liberal, republican, radical, or merely idiosyncratic depends as much on how these terms are defined as upon the person's own words. Theorists may, of course, also change their minds on important issues over time (as the best of us often do), and they can thus be slotted into several different categories at once. What the following account does try to avoid is the assumption that Canadian political thought is a chronological development from one body of thought to another, i.e., the claim that we were all Tories, and then we became enlightened liberals, and we will end up as progressive socialists. It is not difficult to show that examples of different streams of thought coexisted contemporaneously. It *does* stretch credibility, however, to assume that each of these threads was self-contained and unsullied by the influence of the others. (The agrarian movements, for example, were often a potent brew of conflicting principles.) One must also keep in mind that, even in simpler days, political opportunity was as great a motivator as political principle. Given all this, it is hardly surprising that there is such a great deal of controversy over the specific development of political thought in Canada.

TORYISM

Canadians, it is frequently said, find their identity in the fact that they are not Americans; however, "defining Canadians in subtle terms of what they are not," as Conrad Black once shrugged, "is not a compelling rallying cry."[1] Yet it was precisely the venerable tradition of Toryism that Americans most vehemently repudiated in their demand for independence. Americans, one might argue, chose to define *themselves* as a nation against what was a defining feature of Britain's Canadian territories: Toryism. This Tory legacy, many argue, has provided a considerably different focus on political issues within Canada to the present.

The French Revolution, which began in 1789, was perhaps the most emphatic repudiation of the pre-Enlightenment order, and it was precisely in response to the carnage and chaos of the French Revolution that the Anglo-Irish philosopher Edmund Burke wrote his classic defence of conservatism, *Reflections on the Revolution in France*. However, even in 1790, Burke's ideas were considerably out of fashion, and his passionate apology for the conservative world view was considered by many in his day to be little more than a lament for a dying way of life.

Burke was not a reactionary, nor was he a supporter of absolutism in and of itself. Burke was a man of strong principle, and he was known in his day for his castigation of the behaviour of the British East India Company. Burke's opposition to those in power often occurred, however, because he espoused the "traditional rights of Englishmen," which, not infrequently, meant constitutional limits upon the powers of the monarch. Yet he accepted, as French revolutionaries did not, that the very existence of a monarch, in an orderly and predictable succession, provided the political and social stability within which these rights could be enjoyed. Not only stability, he argued, but also the growth and flourishing of a culture were dependent upon a richly layered social order where the successes of the past were able to form the foundation for the achievements of the future. The traditions and rituals of a society were the wine of wisdom distilled through generations of practice, and repudiating these established ways of conduct and belief resulted in a thin and meaningless social existence. Individuals without a sense of their past, he famously stated, were no more than the "flies of summer," which grow and die having achieved nothing, and with little consequence to any other fly. Human beings were special in the eyes of God, but their significance also meant they had particular duties to God and to each other. One of these duties was the observance of a "social contract" between the generations. By presenting respect for the past (and future) generations in contractual terms, Burke was mocking the social contract tradition upon which liberal philosophers justified their principles of conditional obligation. Burke's intergenerational contract was also, however, an effective metaphor to illustrate the importance of cultural and religious continuity through time, which he saw as a linear and progressive movement of generations that distinguished mankind very palpably from the animal world.

Loyalism and Protestantism

Burke's influence in pre-Confederation Canada was arguably more consequential than it was in Britain, and most emphatically so after the United States declared war upon Britain in 1812. The secession of the United States in 1776 had led to a massive influx of loyalists into Canada. Consequently, loyalist sentiment served as the most obvious principle differentiating the two political communities, and loyalty to the Crown played a notable role in the culture of Upper Canada, serving as not only the basis of political legitimacy but also the measure of social acceptability.[2] John Strachan, Anglican bishop for Toronto from 1839 to 1867, is considered to be Canada's first and foremost "High Tory." Strachan stressed loyalty to God and Great Britain and argued that Upper Canada ought formally to recognize the Church of England (the Anglican church) as the established church. As the United States no longer recognized the British monarch as head of church and state, Protestantism began to develop quite different trajectories in Canada and the United States. The argument for the formal recognition of the Church of England in Canada (which was never officially granted) was thus a political as well as a doctrinal strategy, one that sparked great interest from the imperial government.

Tories, though plentiful in Upper Canada, were not limited to that region. The Maritimes too embraced the principles of Toryism in good measure. In Nova Scotia, for example, Thomas Chandler Haliburton wrote both political pamphlets and novels glorifying some of the more sentimental ideals of Burke and warning against the morally corrupt republicanism of the United States. The use of Burkean ideas as a basis for early anti-Americanism made perfect sense in the nineteenth century no less than in the twentieth, although it should be noted that Burke himself was, on principle, not an opponent of the American Revolution, which he saw as substantially different in nature from the French Revolution.

If loyalism was not merely an Upper Canadian phenomenon, neither was it a simple or uniform one. Political elites, for example were much more likely to hold loyalist views and Tory values than those in the lower socio-economic categories.[3] And not all loyalists were British descendants: as the British Crown had facilitated the emigration of many eighteenth-century French and German protestants who faced persecution in Europe, these emigrants and their descendents retained a strong sense of gratitude to Britain. Further, not all loyalists were Anglicans.

Although Tories such as Strachan and Haliburton emphatically presented the link between loyalism and the Church of England, other Canadian Tories challenged it. Challengers accepted that both loyalism to Great Britain and the endorsement of Burkean ideas required the protection of Christianity, but Protestant factionalism diminished the exclusive right of the Church of England to wave the banner of loyalism in the Canadian territories. Egerton Ryerson, a Methodist minister and administrator, articulated a passionate defence of Upper Canada's imperial ties to Great Britain. He had to work much harder than his Anglican compatriots, however, as the Methodist congregations included large numbers of Reformers who were quite sympathetic to American grievances with Britain. Also, as evangelical Protestant movements such as Methodism filled the void in the United States left by the Church of England, many of those in Upper Canada viewed all Methodists with suspicion.

Tradition

Respect for the past is another defining quality of Toryism. This reverence played a much smaller political role than loyalism in pre-Confederation Canada, but its impact was, over time, perhaps more profound. To an extent, loyalism is itself an aspect of the respect for history espoused by Edmund Burke, but the resonance of tradition went well beyond issues of loyalism. Tradition's influence is especially important when considering the role of Lower Canada, with its large French Catholic population. By the nineteenth century, the political status of France in North America was hardly comparable to the threat of American republicanism, and French colonists (including the Acadians who returned after their expulsion from Nova Scotia) were more concerned with maintaining their religion and their language than with preserving any formal political ties with France. Most French settlement had, in any case, occurred well before the French Revolution, and many French settlers were more comfortable with the strictures of feudalism than with the principles of liberalism.

English Tory values, in some cases, often dovetailed quite comfortably with the French Catholic way of life. In the educational outlook of Bishop Strachan, for example, schools were primarily to educate young people—and especially boys—in the Christian virtues. This aim was similar to that of most parochial schools in Lower Canada. The idea of education for the sake of developing a critical intellect was dismissed as unimportant, if not dangerous. Elitism in both communities was accepted, based on the assumption of a natural superiority of intellect by the privileged few.

It is perhaps indicative of the force of "English values" that few Canadian Tories felt the need to catalogue what, precisely, they were. Burke's caricature of the French revolutionaries nonetheless defines what he valued in the English: a civility born out of the medieval codes of chivalry, an aesthetic sensibility that appreciated the sublime, a sense of moderation and measure in action and behaviour, and an acceptance of duty and one's place in the social landscape. Civility, moderation, and deference are not infrequently cited as Canadian qualities. Respect for authority, for example, is quite evident in the Canadian political tradition, and evidence of this deference has ranged from the peaceful opening up of the Canadian West, in comparison to the violence of American frontier settlement, to modern gun laws. The governance made possible by this deference has been described as "benign paternalism" and has, some have argued, meant that Canadian politics have had a tendency to be elite-led. Economic development has, even from the establishment of the national railroad system, often been the project of the respective federal and provincial governments rather than a responsibility of the private sector.

One of the more interesting paradoxes of Toryism in Canada is that the same values and qualities that espoused a culturally chauvinistic and intolerant political culture could morph so fluidly into a society known for its capacity for accommodation. The attitude of cultural elites in nineteenth-century Canada, as in the Canada of the 1950s, was hardly sympathetic to the aboriginal, Black, or even non-British European communities in Canada. The multiculturalism of twenty-first-century Canada did not evolve because Canadians were more kindly or open-minded; most cultural elites in English-speaking Canada glorified British imperialism ("sublime and affecting as it is," wrote Bishop Strachan, "and pregnant with happiness and peace"), while French-Canadian elites demurred only to favour their own form of cultural nationalism.4 To the extent that cultural accommodation was the result of Tory (as opposed to liberal) attitudes at all, it was perhaps to be gleaned from the Tory values of deference (often to liberal elites), moderation, and collective responsibility.

Collectivism

Collectivism is simply the belief that the interests of the group are as important, if not more so, than those of the individuals within it. Thus, many varieties of collectivism exist, and they depend upon different kinds of justifications. The basis for Tory collectivism is the proposition that the individual can only find substantive meaning in his or her life through reference to the larger community. Too much liberty, unconstrained and unstructured, results only in a sordid chaos of self-interest. Individuals become exalted even as the relations between individuals become inconsequential. Thus the customs and rituals of a community, even if they cannot be understood as "rational" principles, are essential in allowing individuals to make sense of who they are and where they come from. Rather than dismissing individuals, Toryism, in this account, allows for the development of richly layered, "situated" individuals who have a sense of "meaningfulness" in their lives.

The reverence for tradition espoused by Tories was, of course, reserved for British customs; the attitudes of colonial elites in Canada were not notably open-minded or cosmopolitan. But the Tory outlook also focused upon the simple organic unity of the society rather than upon the individuals within the society. This outlook found a great deal of resonance in the wide-ranging groups of non-British immigrants who began to populate the Canadian frontier. In the late nineteenth century these groups were largely from southern European and Slavic nations, where liberal values and institutions had not made a considerable impact. Arguably, the tendency to think about the well-being of the group rather than the rights of the individual was an asset in the attempt to survive the hardships of rural homesteading. Many small communities, especially on the prairies, were comprised of numerous cultural enclaves, and the idea of collectivism, although amorphous, was well enough understood to serve as a cultural bridge between immigrant groups.

Collectivism was also a political response to an economic crisis for agricultural producers. Grain was a major cash crop for most prairie farmers in the early twentieth century, but the privately owned grain elevators had an effective monopoly on the market. Isolated rural farmers who had little knowledge of market conditions simply accepted what they were given when they took their product to market, and, as in any condition where one seller exists along with numerous buyers, the market generally favoured the grain operators. This inequity was the source of much Western political discontent. In 1906, the United Grain Growers (UGG) was formed as a response to the monopoly position of the grain merchants, and it (along with the Saskatchewan Wheat Pool) became a significant political force on the prairies. In 1909, the United Farmers of Alberta (UFA) was formed as a political lobby group as well as an economic association and a social organization. While its raison d'être was to promote the economic well-being of farmers (pushing for farm credit programs, irrigation systems, and centralized grain marketing), it was also instrumental in social policy, successfully lobbying for prohibition in 1915 and women's suffrage in 1916. The UFA formed the Alberta government from 1921 to 1935, largely under the guidance of Henry Wise Wood. Wood had developed a unique political theory of government that involved representation on the basis of occupation. An idiosyncratic blend of parliamentary liberalism and guild socialism, Wood's theory of "group government" stipulated that farmers ought to be represented in parliament by a farmers' group, industrial workers by a factory workers' group, and so on. Wood's account never achieved any real political support, but the concept of collectivism in agricultural production—especially in wheat, eggs, and dairy—is still a distinguishing feature of Canadian agriculture in the North American economy.

The history of collectivism in Canada, thus, had a significant economic basis and was, in addition, influenced by a number of factors beyond British Toryism. These include the collectivist tradition of Methodism and the populist alliance movements from the United States (based, as they were, upon ideals of civic republicanism). In some ways, too, the hierarchy and elitism characteristic of British Toryism contradicted (and provoked) the populist sentiment underlying prairie populism. In terms of the development of a broader political culture, however, the various streams of collectivism complemented each other particularly well, providing the basis for a truly *national* sentiment in the twentieth century that, according to many, was palpably distinct from that of the United States.

Toryism in the twentieth century

In 1965, George Parkin Grant wrote his famous eulogy for Toryism in Canada, and, with both resignation and anger, he explained how American values had eclipsed Canadian traditions. Yet the funeral had been a long time in coming: in 1888, his grandfather, George Parkin, had written an equally outraged response to Goldwin Smith's proposal for greater economic integration with the United States. "[I]t seems impossible to conceive," raged Parkin, "how, without a debasement of public sentiment quite unparalleled in history, a people whose history began in loyalty to British institutions, who through a hundred years have been sheltered by British power, who under that rule have attained and enjoyed the most complete political and religious liberty, who have constantly professed the most devoted regard for a mother land with which they are connected by a thousand ties of affectionate sympathy, should deliberately, in cold blood, and for commercial reasons only, break that connection and join themselves to a state in whose history and traditions they have no part."[5]

Anti-Americanism has always been an aspect of Canadian political culture, but it was only in the twentieth century that the expression of anti-Americanism became a clear response to a society built upon the exaltation of individualism, the use of technology, and the force of consumerism. In Canada's geographical and economic vulnerability, Canadians quite quickly became aware of the consequences of this web of modernity.

One of the first to study systematically the impact of technology upon the development of social, political, and economic institutions, Harold Innis recognized that the way in which technological progress unfolded within a particular space had a direct impact upon the manner in which communities grew and changed. Innis was not himself a traditional Tory, but his work, like that of Marshall McLuhan, drew the attention of those twentieth-century Canadians who had begun to experience some dismay over the direction and influence of modern American liberalism. Innis, attempting to construct "a theoretical framework on which the facts of Canadian history could be hung," examined the relationship between the "frontier experience" and changing forms of technology. [6] Beginning with studies on Canada's early "staple products" (fur, minerals, and cod), Innis began to realize that "[t]he effects of geography may be offset by technology.... Geography provides the grooves which determine the course and to a large extent the character of economic life."[7] Communication technology especially interested Innis. In two of Innis's later works, *Empire and Communication* and *The Bias of Communication* (published in 1950 and 1951 respectively), the emphasis was on how the dominant form of communication affected the way in which social relations and institutions were structured. Technology, and especially the technology of communication, was, he argued, the main determinant of social change.

The themes of technology, communication, and culture were examined from a more sociological perspective by Marshall McLuhan, who worked with Innis at the University of Toronto. Following Innis's thesis that human perception was influenced by the *way* in which communication technology delivered ideas and information, McLuhan's book *Understanding Media: The Extensions of Man* (1964) argued that modern societies were shifting from a print form of communication to an electronic one and that the social consequences of this would be enormous. Interestingly, McLuhan's reference was television, as computers were not yet accessible by the mass public, but his ideas can be extended to this domain as well. "The medium," he famously stated, "is the message." In other words, the way in which information reaches us has more profound ramifications than the content of this information itself. The news that we get from newspapers has a different impact upon us than the news we get from television, and the news we access on the Net, we could add, influences us in a different way again. Print media, argued McLuhan, is quite linear; it isolates individuals from each other in their engagement with the written work. But the electronic media is quite different. "Obsession with the older patterns of mechanical, one-way expansion from centres to margins is no longer relevant to our electric world. Electricity does not centralize, but decentralizes."[8]

McLuhan developed a "double dialectic" of technology, observing that for every "extension"(where technology facilitated or assisted in an activity) there would likely be an "amputation" (where technological gains resulted in certain costs). Thus, one might suggest that the prevalence of text messaging undermines the ability to spell correctly, the existence of fast food leads to poor nutrition, and the sophistication of online search engines diminishes the ability of students to undertake library research. Nonetheless, the power of technology has the capacity under the right circumstances to allow us to "retrieve" valued qualities notwithstanding its disadvantages: the widespread use of computers may diminish the amount of time that people devote to reading books or newspapers, yet, if we access the right online sources, we may become *more* literate and cosmopolitan rather than less. However, even the capacity for retrieval can cause a reversal if the technology becomes overextended. Having the technological ability to discover and comprehend how so many people live in poverty and deprivation, for example, may simply drive us to the comfort of anodyne Hollywood movies or lurid detective novels.[9]

Despite McLuhan's early recognition in *The Mechanical Bride* (1951) that the commercialization of mass communication had insidious effects (notably through advertising), he remained ambivalent about the effects of technological change. Much more pessimistic was George Grant, who, like Edmund Burke almost two hundred years earlier, was able to identify what was most important only when it became irretrievably lost. Grant was perhaps the pre-eminent Tory of the twentieth century, but he was also, as one commentator noted, the most anguished one.[10] Like Innis and McLuhan, Grant started with technology. Unlike Innis and

McLuhan, however, who saw technology as a dynamic and complex force, Grant viewed technology as a dark and homogenizing power. Take, for example, the car:

> Canadians wanted the most efficient car for geographic circumstances and social purposes similar to those of the people who first developed the mass-produced automobile. Our desire for and use of such cars has been a central cause of our political and economic integration and our social homogenisation with the people of the imperial heartland. This was not only because of the vast corporate structures necessary for building and keeping in motion such automobiles, and the direct and indirect political power of such corporations, but also because any society with such vehicles tends to become like any other society with the same. Seventy-five years ago somebody might have said "The automobile does not impose on us the ways it should be used", and who would have quarrelled with that? Yet this would have been a deluded representation of the automobile.[11]

The anguish, for Grant, is built upon the realization that technological progress is both inevitable and desirable, as it can ameliorate such undesirable circumstances as "pain, infant mortality, and crop failure." It is not the fact of technological homogenization itself but rather the nature of the homogenization that distresses Grant.

The social vocabulary of technology, he argues, is built upon the discourse of scientific rationality, and what is wrong with scientific rationality is not what it produces but what it leaves out. For in a culture that holds rationality to be the measure of truth, qualities that cannot be measured, classified, and quantified are given little attention or credence. The "noble art of politics," for example, "has turned into technocracy and administration. The tragedy is that man is essentially a political being, and by being deprived of politics he is alienated not only from society but from himself."[12] Thus, what we are left with—and what is exemplified best in American culture and politics—is the glorification of not only technology but also freedom, with little understanding or concern about how best to use it:

> [W]hen we use this language of "freedom" and "values" to ask seriously what substantive "values" our freedom should create, it is clear that such values cannot be discovered in "nature" because in the

light of modern science nature is objectively conceived as indiffer-
ent to value ... Where then does our freedom to create values find
its content?[13]

Where we have traditionally found our moral codes, he reminds us,
has been in our customs and our cultures. Because it grounded
Canadian values, the Tory tradition was very important to Grant, and,
consequently, he feared the gradual encroachment of the American
way of life on Canadian society. Grant was a student of classics and
theology; and for most of his life he was dismissed as "not a real
philosopher" by those who were. However, it was precisely within classical writings and the Christian tradition that humans could find their
social and moral compass; philosophy, to him, was part of the problem, as it taught us to be clever thinkers, but would not tell us to what
we ought to set our minds. We have gained mastery over our physical world, he concluded, but we have lost touch with the sublime,
the transcendent, and the virtuous. We are lost on a web of direc-
tionless and bleak concrete freeways, but—well, we drive great cars.

BRITISH LIBERALISM AND CONSTITUTIONALISM

The British stream of liberal thought that permeated Canadian
political values can easily be confused with the stream of American
liberalism that put its faith in the strength of laws and constitutions
over inchoate traditions to preserve stability and liberty in modern
societies. This confusion is possible because both British and
American constitutionalism evolved originally from many of the
same sentiments and principles articulated in late seventeenth-
century Britain. The key difference between the two accounts rests
in the approach of each to the achievement of freedom from arbitrary coercion: those in the American liberal tradition thought that
freedom was to be attained in the absence of monarchical rule while
those in the British tradition believed that freedom was best secured
within in. The early British Whig hostility to arbitrary rule by the
Crown was a reaction to the restrictions imposed by Charles I and
James II, who both attempted to limit the traditional rights of the
people and thus precipitated, respectively, the English Civil War
and the Glorious Revolution of 1688.

The dissatisfaction expressed by American colonists against British colonial rule was neither of short duration nor passively articulated, and many influential British thinkers (including Burke) suggested that transferring more powers to American colonists might forestall more extreme political measures. This advice was not taken, and it is not surprising that, faced with similar sentiments emanating from the Canadian colonies some decades later, the British government was more receptive to a more liberal compromise. Also, by the 1830s, the British government was itself in a position to be more magnanimous: its political relationships with both France and America had stabilized, and the internal politics of Great Britain had taken a decidedly liberal turn, which included significant social reforms (including the expansion of suffrage and the formal abolition of slavery).

However, if the monarchy survived in Canada for largely practical reasons, there was nonetheless a resonant theory of government, quite distinct from the American model, which underpinned it. American liberalism is unrepentantly Lockean, that is to say, it was grounded upon the principles of social contract theory and natural right most clearly articulated by John Locke in his *Treatises of Government*. Political obligation is based not upon traditional practice but upon individual consent, and consent is only given as long as a state acts in the clear interests of its citizens. But British liberalism is based upon a more opaque reference to an eminent set of traditions and institutions that recognize the historical rights of Englishmen. Locke had catalogued many of the defects of this traditional system.[14] Yet, sentimentalism aside, the British parliamentary system had in fact evolved into an exemplary system of governance that promoted the safeguards of civil liberties. The "noble rights of Englishmen" included the requirements of habeas corpus, trial by jury, and other protections found in English Common Law; also, the structure of English political institutions, as the French theorist Montesquieu explained, were limited by the balance of power distributed between Crown, aristocracy, and church. "Empire," wrote historian W.L. Morton, "was held to be compatible with liberty, and liberty was guaranteed by the obligation of monarchical government to maintain the inherited rights of its subjects."[15]

Not all Canadians accepted the argument that political liberties were best protected within a tradition of monarchism. Upper Canada at the beginning of the nineteenth century had a large population of American immigrants and refugees, and American political ideas as well as religious doctrines strongly contested traditional British ones. American republicanism was an obvious alternative to British constitutionalism, a point that many early reformers in Canada stressed quite emphatically. Throughout the first half of the nineteenth century, however, an enormous wave of British immigration, supplemented by the concerted effort of the Church of England to solidify its position against the evangelical movements, stemmed the tide of support for republicanism. "Responsible government" was the Canadian compromise between monarchical rule and self-representation, and it required that the executive branch of government be responsible to the elected representatives of the people. In other words, it transferred a substantial level of power from the Queen's appointed representative in the colonies to an elected Legislative Assembly. Although the institution of responsible government was, of course, one of the primary recommendations of Lord Durham's 1839 Report, it had been a reform that politicians in Upper Canada had attempted to secure for some time. As Robert Baldwin warned in 1836,

I take it for granted that Great Britain cannot desire to exercise a Government of the sword, and that she will therefore only govern the Canadas so long as she can do so with the concurrence of the People—For the purpose therefore of continuing the connexion upon this footing it is absolutely necessary; First—That the political machinery of the Provincial Government should be such, as shall work harmoniously within itself, without collision between any of its great wheels; And secondly, That it should be such as that the People may feel that they have an influence upon it sufficiently powerful to secure attention, not only to their abstract rights, but to their feelings and Prejudices; without regard to these you can govern no people satisfactorily or successfully.[16]

The principle of responsible government was established in 1848, but it led to further intractable problems. Because maintaining a majority government in the newly configured Executive Council proved difficult, governments consistently fell soon after they were formed, and the resulting political instability precipitated negotiations culminating in Confederation in 1867.

Nevertheless, the legacy of this compromise remains substantial. In Canada the *legal* sovereignty, which rests in the Crown, is independent of the *political* sovereignty, which resides in the national Parliament (and, by extension, in the people of Canada). This divided sovereignty means that "the last essential of government, the maintenance of peace and order," as W.L. Morton argues, remains "independent of popular impulse."[17] This sentiment, of course, is exemplified by the Canadian Senate, the House of "sober second thought," which at its institution was seen as a hedge against rash and capricious populism. The institutional structure of Canada is thus grounded upon the principles of moderation. More important, however, is the claim that the monarchical influence "allowed a diversity of customs and rights under law in a way that the rational scheme and abstract principles of republican democracy did not."[18] The American liberal tradition was appealing for a great number of reasons (as Louis Papineau in his "Six Counties Address" provocatively emphasized), but it was also emphatic in its insistence that citizens were, in essence, equal in both their natural rights and their fungibility. British liberalism, while cognizant of the need to respect civil liberties, never attempted to dislocate individuals from their social fabric:

> The monarchy, in short, subsumed a heterogeneous and conservative society governed in freedom under law, law upheld by monarchy, where the republic would have levelled the diversities and made uniform the various groups by breaking them down into individuals, free indeed, but bound by social conformity and regimented by an inherent social intolerance.[19]

The British liberal tradition in the twentieth century

In his acerbic reflections on the liberal tradition in Canada, published in 1960, Frank Underhill wrote that the most notable feature of modern liberal thought in Canada was its absence:

> ... the most notable illustration of this poverty of our politics at the intellectual level is to be found in the fact that while we were the pioneers in one of the great liberal achievements of the nineteenth

century—the experiment of responsible government, which transformed the British Empire into the Commonwealth, and which has
thrown fresh light in our own day on the possibility of reconciling
nationalism with a wider international community—even in this field,
in which our practical contribution was so great, there has arisen
since the days of Joseph Howe no Canadian prophet of the idea of
the Commonwealth whose writings seem inspiring or even readable
to wider circles than those of professional historians.[20]

This statement is not inaccurate, but it is perhaps a little harsh
because, precisely at the time Underhill was writing, Canadian liberalism began to take a distinctive shape.

From Confederation in 1867 and for the next hundred years,
liberalism in Canada was a largely pragmatic exercise, but a significant success nonetheless. One of the biggest issues of Confederation
was whether the proposed state of Canada ought to be a *legislative*
union, in which a central authority formulated and administered
the laws, or a *federal* union, where a significant proportion of the
laws were made at the regional level, and only those matters of a
clearly national focus would be determined by at a federal level. The
Civil War in the United States was manifest proof of the dangers of
federalism, but the approval of Quebec and the Maritime colonies
was only secured by guaranteeing regional control over local matters.
This guarantee was, of course, especially important to Quebec, with
its distinct linguistic and religious orientation.

Quebec, however, was also very much influenced by its feudal past
and its Roman Catholic present. It was the pragmatic but significant
achievement of Prime Minister Wilfrid Laurier to shift the political
orientation of Quebec to the liberalism of early twentieth-century
Britain. The conservatism of early Quebec and the liberalism Laurier
espoused were not hopelessly divergent. Unlike the laissez-faire liberalism dominant in the United States at the time, the "New Liberalism"
of the British intellectuals argued for a greater role for the state in
achieving the best possible conditions for individuals. The New
Liberalism movement was set into motion at the end of the nineteenth century by T.H. Green, a British idealist, who, influenced by
Hegelian thought, argued that the state should play a key role in
constructing an environment in which individuals could more effectively make moral choices. The abstract moral philosophy of Green's

thought was applied more concretely to political concerns by L.T. Hobhouse and J.A. Hobson, who both argued that poverty and social reform were the proper responsibility of a more involved state.

The liberalism of Laurier was a practical liberalism, for Laurier was obliged to deal with intransigent issues of national unity throughout his long term in office. The protection of language rights in the public school system, for example, was one of his lasting achievements. Another was the development of the West—no small matter, as the agricultural interests of western farmers (much like today) conflicted directly with the manufacturing interests of central Canada and the ethnic composition of western settlement hardly reflected the demographic character of the East.

Britain's New Liberalism had a much more direct impact upon Prime Minister William Lyon Mackenzie King. King, who had been Laurier's Minister of Labour until 1911, had a long-standing interest in labour relations. Factory conditions in the twentieth century were not well regulated, and King was frequently appalled at the problems he witnessed. In his 1918 book *Industry and Humanity*, King argued that the state had a right and a responsibility to become more involved in the control of capital. Yet the King era was notable not for industrial relations but for social welfare policy. It is true that much of King's progressivism was reactive: he was, for example, faced with the Depression of the 1930s, the rise of radical political movements, the rejection by the courts of the attempt to use federal legislation to address social welfare, and the need to establish effective demobilization policies following World War II. He also was presented with new tools to use in thinking through these crises (most particularly in John Maynard Keynes's economic theories and William Henry Beveridge's roadmap for modern social welfare in Britain). But King did achieve significant political successes nonetheless: he negotiated federal-provincial plans with the provinces to establish old age pensions (1926) and unemployment insurance (1940), and he oversaw Canada's blueprint for its modern welfare system, the *Report on Social Security for Canada* (1943).

By 1960, when Underhill cast words of aspersion upon Canadian liberalism, Canadian liberalism had clearly begun to take shape. This was the liberalism of moderation. As Lester B. Pearson declared in a speech given in 1953 to the Ontario Liberal Association,

Liberalism, because it has always believed in and fought for freedom, stands for another principle of vital importance today: moderation, tolerance, and the rejection of extreme courses, whether they come from the right or the left....

This middle way, the liberal way, has positive faith in the common sense of the great majority of the people. It relies on their intelligence, their will to cooperate, and their sense of justice. Its strength is that of tolerance and restraint. It rests on the discipline of mind rather than muscle, and on the belief that human problems, vast and complicated though they may be, are capable of solutions. This, I believe, is the political philosophy which can best preserve a free society in Canada.[21]

The economic aspects of moderation and tolerance are still visible in the contrast between the social welfare systems of Canada and the United States, although, as Tuohy has observed, the distinction rests largely upon the role of Canadian health care and not upon social programmes per se.[22] Also, when contrasted to that of most European states, Canada's economic generosity becomes noticeably less distinctive.

The real measure of modern Canadian liberalism has been in its practical (and, more recently, its philosophical) application of social tolerance to the arena of intercultural relations. Gay marriage and the legalization of marijuana may be distinctive Canadian features when compared to the United States, but they would not elicit any gasps of shock or admiration from citizens of, say, the Netherlands. What is more idiosyncratic is that, unlike states that have been culturally homogeneous historically, Canada has been able to achieve such liberal policies despite, and possibly even because of, its historical ethnic diversity.

The political significance of historical efforts to accommodate Quebec (and of resistance to those efforts) should, of course, be tempered by the recognition that an expansive definition of human rights was not a priority in Canada until fairly recently. The onerous restrictions against Chinese immigrant labourers (including the notorious head tax), the lukewarm response to Jewish refugees, the internment of Japanese-Canadian citizens, Quebec's Padlock Act against communists, and various legislation vis-à-vis aboriginal groups are concrete instances of less than tolerant social attitudes.[23] Still, by the middle of the twentieth century, a number of liberal-minded scholars were becoming quite vocal about the deficiencies of Canadian legislation and especially about the lack of an entrenched Charter of Rights. Diefenbaker's 1960 Bill of Rights was a start, argued jurists like Frank Scott, "[b]ut it is a very partial Bill, applicable only in peacetime, no stronger than the self-restraint of our federal members of Parliament at any given moment, and inapplicable to provincial legislatures."[24] After considerable discussion and negotiation, and no little acrimony, the Constitution Act, containing an entrenched Charter of Rights, became a reality in 1982. Critics worried that the Charter, which permitted the courts to disallow any legislation deemed to violate specified human rights, was modelled on the American system of judicial rather than parliamentary supremacy and would make Canadian politics "too American."

However, the Charter was very distinct from its American counterpart in a number of ways, the most important being "provisions offering explicit protection for the rights of minorities, provisions that reflect twentieth-century notions of human rights and fundamental freedoms":

> The rights of both of Canada's great linguistic communities have been recognized in the Constitution and the Charter. The special place of the Native Peoples—the Indians, the Inuit and the Metis—has been acknowledged. We have also acknowledged the multicultural dimension of Canadian society, and another provision of the Charter ... guarantee[s] to every individual the right of equality under the law and the right to the equal protection of the law "without discrimination based on race, national or ethnic origin, [or] colour."[25]

In contrast with Toryism, then, the British "Whig" tradition of liberalism in Canada emphasized an uneasy concern with the possibilities of arbitrary power residing in an executive authority with little or no formal checks. Britain had faced her own crisis of authority in the seventeenth century and had come to a stable resolution of it through the establishment of a constitutional monarchy. But Britain's American colonies, while governed in principle under the same British laws, were subject to discrete laws imposed by Britain over which they had little say (the most infamous being the 1765 Stamp Act). Thus, the same issue arose again: did the colonial authority have sufficient checks upon it to make it responsive to the people who were directly subject to it? The response of the thirteen rebelling American colonies was a clear "no," and the accounts given by American revolutionaries argued that the imperial bond itself had prohibited American liberty.

In contrast, moderates in the Canadian colonies came to realize that, with the disparate composition of its population (including a large French population and a significant number of American-inspired republicans), political stability could be reconciled with local accountability through a system of responsible government within the imperial system. Thus the principle of greater state presence in political affairs has generally been tolerated in Canadian politics. What this has meant in its contemporary manifestation is that matters of a "merely private nature"—such as health care or cultural traditions—can appeal more easily to the state for recognition and protection because of the principle that the state has a valid role beyond the protection of basic liberties.

NOTES

1 Conrad Black, "Perspectives on Canada from an ex-citizen," Inaugural T. Patrick Boyle Founders Lecture, Fraser Institute, Vancouver, 15 Nov. 2001.
2 For a more detailed study, see David Mills, *The Concept of Loyalty in Upper Canada, 1784-1850* (Kingston and Montreal: McGill-Queen's University Press, 1988).
3 See, for example, Edward Grabb and James Curtis, *Regions Apart: The Four Societies of Canada and the United States* (Don Mills, ON: Oxford University Press, 2005) 83–86.
4 John Strachan, "On Church establishment," *Canadian Political Thought*, ed. H.D. Forbes (Toronto: Oxford University Press, 1985) 15.
5 Sir George Parkin, "The reorganization of the British Empire," *Canadian Political Thought*, ed. H.D. Forbes (Toronto: Oxford University Press, 1985) 163.
6 Robin Neill, *A New Theory of Value: The Canadian Economics of H.A. Innis* (Toronto: University of Toronto Press, 1972) 43–44.
7 Harold Innis "On the economic significance of culture," quoted in Neill, *A New Theory of Value* 43–44.
8 Marshall McLuhan, *Understanding Media: The Extensions of Man* (New York: McGraw-Hill, 1964) 36.
9 For a discussion of McLuhan's "tetrad" see Todd Kappelman, "Marshall McLuhan: 'The medium is the message,'" *Probe Ministries International*, 2001, *Leadership U Telling the Truth Project*, 16 Sept. 2005 <http://www.leaderu.com/orgs/probe/docs/mcluhan.html>.
10 John Muggeridge, "Grant's anguished conservatism," *George Grant in Process*, ed. Larry Schmidt (Toronto: Anansi Press, 1978) 40–48.
11 George Grant "Thinking about technology," *Technology and Justice* (Toronto: Anansi Press, 1986) 24.
12 A. James Reimer, "George Grant: liberal, socialist, or conservative?" *George Grant in Process* 55.
13 George Grant "In defence of North America," *Technology and Empire* (Toronto: Anansi Press, 1969) 33.

[14] See Annabel Patterson, *Early Modern Liberalism* (Cambridge: Cambridge University Press, 1997).

[15] W.L. Morton, "The relevance of Canadian history," Presidential address to the Canadian Historical Association, Queen's University, 11 June 1960, 16 Sept. 2005 <http://www.cha-shc.ca/bilingue/addresses/1960.htm>.

[16] Robert Baldwin, "Letter written to Lord Glenelg, Colonial Secretary, 1836," *Canadian Political Thought*, ed. H.D. Forbes (Toronto: Oxford University Press, 1985) 126–33.

[17] Morton, "The relevance of Canadian history" 10.

[18] Morton, "The relevance of Canadian history" 10.

[19] Morton, "The relevance of Canadian history" 10.

[20] Frank Underhill, *In Search of Canadian Liberalism* (Toronto: Macmillan, 1960) 7.

[21] Lester B. Pearson, *Words and Occasions* (Toronto: University of Toronto Press, 1970) 122.

[22] Carolyn Hughes Tuohy, "Social policy: two worlds," *Governing Canada: Institutions and Public Policy*, ed. Michael Atkinson (Toronto: Harcourt Brace Jovanovich, 1993).

[23] See, for example, Reg Whitaker, *Double Standard: The Secret History of Canadian Immigration* (Toronto: Lester and Orphen Dennys, 1987).

[24] F.R. Scott, *Civil Liberties and Canadian Federalism* (Toronto: University of Toronto Press, 1959) 56.

[25] The Honourable Thomas R. Berger, "Towards the regime of tolerance," *Political Thought in Canada*, ed. Stephen Brooks (Toronto: Irwin Publishing, 1984) 86.

CHAPTER 4

THE CHALLENGE OF
NEIGHBOURLINESS

THE UNITED STATES

The United States has been a cornerstone in the evolution of Canada's political thought, both in the ideas it has espoused and in the threats that it represents. It is difficult to talk about the influence of American political thought insofar as the political ideas developed within the United States have been quite diverse. The writings of Jefferson, Hamilton, and Madison concerning the proper role of a central government, for example, are still considered classic statements of the development of American liberalism. The early American political debates are remarkable, too, for their sophistication and nuance. How can one balance a minimal state with the concern for equality between citizens? How can a liberal democracy protect against the thoughtlessness of a zealous majority? Many of these discussions—especially those concerning the relationship between democracy and federalism—influenced Canadian political debate in the early nineteenth century. However, the stream of American thought that had the greatest impact upon Canada was probably one of the most roughly hewn (but politically popular) creations of American liberalism.

This current, often referred to as "Jacksonian liberalism," is certainly not an uncommon ideological position in Canada, where it became known in the 1980s as the "New Right." Still, this contemporary form of market-oriented liberalism in Canada (often labelled "classical liberalism" or "neo-liberalism") was to a large extent the result of the triumph of the New Right internationally. The pronouncements of Reagan and Thatcher in the 1980s, along with the perception during that decade that Canada's economic well-being might well be linked to its success at winning international markets, became entrenched in Canada with the Conservative government under Brian Mulroney. Yet this variant of liberalism has existed in Canada for as long as Canada itself has existed. Marginalized as "regional sentiment," market liberalism developed its own form in western Canada, and most evidently in Alberta. This manifestation of liberalism was largely the result of the West's own political development (and of its testy political relationship with central Canada), but it was also consistently influenced by the ideological trends evolving in the United States. In addition, significantly, modern Canadian radicalism emerged in response to Jacksonian liberalism. Old-school Tories and left-wing radicals, for example, formed a curious coalition in the late sixties and seventies in response to this form of American liberalism. The most remarkable evidence of this coalition was the courting of George Grant by the New Democratic Party after the publication of Grant's *Lament for a Nation*; neither Grant's vocal position on the abortion debate nor his support for a classical university education seemed to daunt the Left in its quest for Grant's public endorsement.

Stressing the wide variety of American political thought is important. In addition to the plurality of liberalisms developed within the United States, for example, a thriving conservative stream of intellectual thought can be identified, and the American Left had a palpable influence on the early development of Canadian socialism.[1] However, the philosophical nuances of these American political theorists had, unsurprisingly, much less influence upon the development of Canadian thought than did the vociferous proponents of Jacksonian liberalism. One reason for its influence was the relative success that this liberalism enjoyed within the United States itself; another is that it contrasted so emphatically with the political ideas upon which so much of Canadian society was grounded.

JACKSONIAN LIBERALISM AND THE FREE MARKET

When the United States declared its independence from Britain in 1776, its political reference point was the same opposition to arbitrary rule articulated by *British* liberals in the late seventeenth century. The British Whigs, though, generally accepted the principle of a constitutional monarchy while the American republicans did not. The new American state was founded clearly upon principles of democracy. Republicanism, however, is not simply reducible to democracy, and human sentiments do not change as quickly as political institutions can. The new American state remained populated by a significant number of "republican aristocrats" whose support for the ideals of democracy and universal suffrage were, at best, ambivalent. Particularly in the established north-eastern American states, the republican elite seemed to exhibit many traits of Toryism. For them, a well-schooled class of virtuous gentlemen seemed an obvious, natural governing elite, and the nascent state viewed this same class as the most efficient means of securing economic development. Suspicious of populist sentiment and favoured by the government's economic policies, the moneyed aristocracy of early America thus became the focus of increasing resentment.

The anti-populism of the republican elite was not remarkable given the context of late eighteenth-century political developments. The destruction and demoralization wrought by the French Revolution made suspicion of democracy a reasonable attitude, and the lack of infrastructure in the American West seemed to underscore the efficiency of concentrating economic development in the East. Nonetheless, by the 1820s, a widespread dissatisfaction was being expressed by people within a broad coalition of interests; they argued that the economic and political developments being pursued by the old elites did not result in equitable outcomes or opportunities. This opposition solidified around a colourful individual who had won a reputation as a straight-talking "man of the people" with no fancy credentials except as an "Indian fighter" and anti-imperialist. The political movement led by Andrew Jackson gained a great deal of popular support in its call to end the economic and political domination enjoyed by the wealthy and well-connected elites. The strategy of this movement was to promote both an open market in which all propertied individuals could compete fairly and a political domain in which all (white) males exercised equal rights regardless of property ownership.

Jacksonian liberalism, with its call to expand the franchise and to wrest political control away from established elites, became the prototype for the modern Democratic Party, although its emphasis upon the free market and its disinterest in racial reforms also, rather paradoxically, made it the forerunner of the modern Republican Party. By the middle of the nineteenth century, American politics shifted into a different set of political cleavages, and Jacksonian liberalism, as a clear political movement, disappeared. But market liberalism itself took a clearer shape in the nine-

teenth century in response to two developments: political expansionism and the importation of "Manchester School" principles
from Great Britain. The doctrine of "manifest destiny" expressed
in the early 1800s was both an attempt to protect the political sovereignty of the United States and, later, a strategy to secure both raw
goods and markets for its expanding economy. Canada was, of
course, quite influenced by these articulations of continentalism.
Most political expressions in Canada were clearly those of opposition, although some people, such as Goldwin Smith, argued that
"Canadian nationality being a lost cause, the ultimate union of
Canada with the United States appears now to be morally certain;
so that nothing is left for Canadian patriotism but to provide that
it shall be a union indeed, and not an annexation."[2] That Goldwin
Smith was also an enthusiastic proponent of the Manchester School
was not coincidental.

The Manchester School was a term used to refer to Britain's free
trade movement in the nineteenth century. In 1836, the original
focus of the Manchester theorists (Richard Cobden and John
Bright) was to convince the British government to repeal the British
Corn Laws, which were government regulations on the sale of grain,
an important staple food. The Manchester School later became a
reference point for all laissez-faire economic theory, and it fit well
with the emphasis upon free enterprise capitalism in the United
States. But early nineteenth-century America, as historians have
noted, "*was* already the liberal's dream": state regulation of the
economy was quite minimal, and a great deal of small-scale enterprise comprised much of the economic activity. The peculiar
American expression of market liberalism in the *late* nineteenth
century, however, was the attempt of large monopoly corporations
to use these sentiments to enhance their economic influence:

Destitute farmers, ruined craftsmen and legions of immigrants were
asked to surrender their dreams of property-ownership and independence, bow their heads and march quietly into the ranks of an
industrial "army" under the command of self-styled "captains of industry" like Vanderbilt, Gould, Carnegie, Mellon, Rockefeller,
Guggenheim ... They had to explain to traditional America, still very
puritanical, how the unrestrained greed, predatory practices and
ostentatious displays of wealth by the "robber barons" could still be

ethical. And, to a population that had only a century earlier fought a revolution against British mercantilist practices, the apologists had to explain why an almost openly-corrupt government should be allowed to use its power to crush trade unions and farmer organizations, place strict controls on the money supply, use regulations to minimize competition among the corporations and throw up trade barriers to coddle them.³

It is instructive to note that the large Canadian companies of the early twentieth century, far from sharing this laissez-faire outlook, held an almost paternalist view of their role in Canadian society. (To a large extent this attitude was held because so many of the early Canadian magnates—Timothy Eaton, Robert Simpson, and Hart Massey—were Methodists, and their businesses were conducted within the larger mandate of improving the social and moral well-being of their communities.)

The American liberalism of the late nineteenth and early twentieth century was clearly beginning to diverge from British liberalism, which had begun to think about how the state could be employed to improve the material welfare of its citizens. The free-market variant that has always been quite pronounced in the United States (even during the height of Keynesianism) has been defined by an emphasis upon limited government, the extensive negative rights of citizens, the balance of power between government institutions, and (at least formally) the separation of church and state. Political thought in the United States in the twentieth century was, to a large extent, defined by economic theory. The dominant economic school for most of that century has been the Chicago School. While the "early" Chicago School (around 1920 to1950) was not altogether unsympathetic to the principle of government intervention in the economy when needed, the second incarnation of the Chicago School actively targeted the principles of Keynesian economics, which had been dominant internationally (though less so in the United States) since the end of the Second World War. The most famous proponent of the Chicago School during this period, Milton Friedman, strongly advocated the principles of neo-classical laissez-faire economics (which became known as monetarism.) Friedman's supply-side economics, which did not gain much popularity during the 1960s and 1970s, eventually became the new orthodoxy under the Reagan administration in the 1980s and served as the economic justification for the administration's call to "roll back the welfare state." But the political philosophy of the minimal state perhaps rested more firmly upon the writings of Friedrich von Hayek who, along with Ludwig von Mises, waged another ideological battle against Keynesianism. Although Hayek worked at the University of Chicago between 1950 and 1962, he was only tangentially involved with Chicago School, yet his best-known works, *The Road to Serfdom* (1944) and *The Constitution of Liberty* (1960), were instrumental in defining the political risks of a state actively involved in economic decision making.

At the national level, Canada was noticeably unaffected by neo-classical economics until the late 1980s. In fact, the economic theories that had the most impact upon policy making at this time were those urging greater state intervention in order to enhance economic and industrial output (during the 1940s and 1950s) and to counter ever-increasing American direct investment in the Canadian economy (during the 1970s and 1980s). These policies made perfect economic sense to those confronted by the issues of the day. However, as the sociologist S.D. Clark has written, state-driven economic development has also been a large component of Canadian political culture. In his classic analysis of the historical development of Canadian political values, Clark explains how the ever-present threat of American expansionism meant that the Canadian colonies were settled under the close supervision of the British military and later, in the West, by the North West Mounted Police. "The result," he states, "was to establish a tradition of respect for the institutions of law and order."[4] Consequently, what had begun as a military strategy protecting political sovereignty progressed as an economic policy, for, while the Americans saw their economy as based upon the "condition of competition," Canada's was grounded upon the existence of monopolistic control:

Here the long reach of the St. Lawrence waterways system into the centre of the continent, and the island character of the Maritime region, early made possible the restriction of competition, with the consequence that the maintenance of monopolistic conditions of control through state intervention became a primary end of business, ecclesiastical, educational, and other such interests. Individual enterprise from the very beginning represented a threat to the developing structure of Canadian economic, political, cultural, and religious life. To a very large extent, as a result, what middle class has grown up in the country has been one developing within a bureaucratic order.[5]

Clark's analysis, while generally sound, is deficient in its assumption that it could be applied to the country as an undifferentiated whole. Clark and other Canadian intellectuals of the period (including Northrop Frye) based their analyses of Canadian political culture upon the "Laurentian thesis," an account constructed by historian Donald Creighton in *The Empire of the St Lawrence*. Originally written in 1937, the book was republished in 1956 as a response to Canadian continentalists, such as Goldwin Smith and Frank Underhill, who argued that, as the natural trade flows in North America ran north and south, there was little economic justification for Canada to exist as a sovereign entity. Creighton argued that the St. Lawrence provided a natural east-west axis from which grew a sense of national unity.

Unfortunately, this romantic sentiment neglects the geographic fact that the St. Lawrence simply does not exist beyond Ontario. The concept of a Laurentian thesis as a basis for national unity, as Barry Cooper flatly states, "is nonsense. There is no Laurentian feeling in British Columbia. The dim memories of such a feeling on the prairies are mostly hostile."[6] Western Canada, to a significant degree, does not share the political culture of the rest of English-speaking Canada. This statement is almost a truism: one has only to read the morning paper to be told that the attitudes of western Canadians are distinct on policy issues, including gun control, the privatization of health care, and Senate reform. In Alberta, especially, the influence of American ideas has remained dominant from the province's settlement up to the present.

One might object that Alberta's historical flirtation with collectivism contradicts the claim of American influence. It is true that populism was a phenomenon throughout the western provinces, but the reason for its strength was that collective behaviour was one of the few political strategies capable of countering the economic and political power of established (frequently monopolistic) commercial interests, which, for historical reasons, were generally based in central

Canada. One must also recognize that populism had both right-wing and left-wing variants, and the prairie radicalism of the twentieth century was, in Alberta, firmly based upon the former.

The establishment of the United Farmers' Association (UFA) as a formal political force in Alberta was quite clearly a "radical" movement and, on first glance, one informed by socialist ideas. Both Henry Wise Wood and William Irvine, its founders, saw that society could be divided into classes, and both believed that competitive behaviour could and ought to be replaced by a form of cooperative activity. Wood, like Irvine (and most other prairie radicals), was informed by the sense of injustice manifest in the exploitation of the independent commodity producers in the west by the commercial interests in the heartland. Yet Wood's political analysis, which formed the ideological backdrop for UFA activism, "stayed within the liberal assumptions in attributing this exploitation not at all to the command of capital over the labour of the many consequent on the divorce of labour from the means of labour, but solely to the unfair competitive strength of some producers in the commodity markets."[7] A deep wariness of party politics had led the UFA to implement a system of delegate democracy, although, as C.B. Macpherson observed in his magisterial study of Albertan democracy, both the UFA and its successor, the Social Credit Party (and, one could add, the modern Progressive Conservative Party), became, in practice, deeply conservative in outlook and considerably centralized in decision making. The quasi-radical character of the quasi-party system, argues Macpherson, was due to the failure of political leaders to jettison their support for an economic system based upon private property: the radicalism of these parties was "that of a quasi-colonial society of independent producers, in rebellion against eastern imperialism, but not against the property system."[8] Alberta politics were always the politics of radicalism, but, as Macpherson notes, this radicalism always had a very conservative underpinning.

Certainly, the refusal of western political movements to accept the political culture of loyalist Canada stems largely from the history of exploitation and subordination experienced by a community (still) predominantly comprised of independent commodity producers. Early development of the West was driven primarily by "rent extraction," which was done at the behest of eastern commercial interests with little concern for the small local settlements. Later generations of farmers and ranchers were doomed by two facts: first, their economic interests generally conflicted directly with those of eastern industrialists and, second, the population base supporting industrial Canada was substantially larger than that of the West. Still, why would that necessarily entail a *market*-based form of political radicalism? Barry Cooper has written that "private property and individual entrepreneurship were a consequence of frontier necessities and established legal institutions, not psychological traits of rugged individualism."[9] True enough; however, this statement begs the question of why a doctrine based on private property rights was deemed superior to one based upon active state involvement. Saskatchewan, for example, was willing to use the provincial government to develop its resources (through the agencies of the Saskatchewan Wheat Board, SaskOil, and the Potash Corporation of Saskatchewan). Alberta rejected this strategy, preferring instead to depend upon private foreign direct investment to develop its petroleum resources even though, in the eyes of some analysts, the use of a Crown corporation to develop the oil industry may well have been a more efficient option.[10]

A more direct explanation for Albertans' consistent support for the principles of American market liberalism may be simply that, historically, a far greater proportion of Americans lived in Alberta than in any other region in Canada. After the last agricultural frontiers in the United States had been "staked and settled" in the 1890s, explains Nelson Wiseman, "Americans poured over the border in Alberta and western Saskatchewan." In 1911, for example, "American-born Albertans outnumbered the British-born; Canadian-born Albertans were in a minority":

> The early sway of Ontario liberalism was soon overshadowed and fused with the more dynamic liberal populism of the Americans. Americans and their ideas shaped provincial politics because they settled in the rural areas. In contrast, the immigrant British-working-class wave gravitated toward the politically underrepresented cities. The Americans espoused a populist rural liberalism, one uninfected by toryism, one more radical and plebiscitarian.[11]

The historical manifestation of American liberal traits was reinforced by the economic ties forged by Alberta within the development of the wheat, ranching, and oil industries throughout the twentieth century. Saskatchewan, in contrast, had higher numbers of British settlers in rural areas, as well as non-English-speaking European immigrants, who formed enough of a critical mass to support a strong socialist tradition.

Yet the political culture of Alberta, like that of much of the United States, is a curious combination of market liberalism and the values of evangelical, fundamental Protestantism. Thus, support for private property and market-oriented policy solutions is traversed with a greater deference to authority, a stronger devotion to traditional institutions (such as family and church), and a clear endorsement of "codes of conduct such as duty and propriety."[12] While free-market liberalism would seem for reasons of consistency to coincide with a laissez-faire approach to social norms, it is not uncommon (especially in the United States) to find supporters of market liberalism also sanctioning state involvement in moral issues (such as opposition to single-sex marriage and abortion, or support for the teaching of creationism in public schools). This conjunction of respect for individual privacy and loyalty to community traditions explains why Alberta is the strongest opponent of gun regulation—gun ownership is a private matter—but also the most vocal opponent of same-sex marriage—the union of two consenting same-sex adults goes against traditional practices and should *not* be merely a private matter. The tension between these two manifestations of right-wing thought also explains dramatic policy shifts over time (and why, for example, a province strongly supporting temperance historically could later become a strong proponent of the deregulation of the sale of alcohol). Interesting, too, is that, in some cases, the political values derived from American fundamentalism dovetail quite nicely with traditional Tory values, such as belief in the importance of God and Church.[13]

In sum, then, the stream of American liberalism based largely on the principles of individualism and a minimal state has been a consistent, if geographically marginalized, current within Canadian political thought. The contemporary fashionableness of neo-liberalism over traditional Canadian Toryism is quite evident in, for example, the merger of the shrinking Progressive Conservative Party of Canada with the largely Alberta-based Reform (and then Alliance) Party. Does this indicate a convergence of values between the two countries? Pollster Michael Adams argues that "we find a picture of startling dissimilitude, and—even more striking—ongoing divergence" between Canadian and American values. In fact, he states, the *average* position of *all* Canadian responses "falls in almost exactly the same spot as the average position of the most progressive social values segment in America."[14] If it is true, then it is quite remarkable that the stream of Canadian political thought addressing the threat that America poses to Canadians—the argument for sovereignty—has become so muted.

THE IDEA OF "SOVEREIGNTY" IN CANADIAN POLITICAL THOUGHT

The fundamental and rather fascinating character of "sovereignty" in Canadian political thought is that it is the product of an unsteady alliance between those supporting Tory principles and those promoting socialist or social-democratic ones. To a certain extent, thinking about sovereignty issues has been a division of labour between those concerned about economic domination (the Left) and those anxious about cultural domination (the Tories), but both groups have tended to recognize that cultural and economic sovereignty are, for the most part, interdependent. This tentative and often begrudging alliance between the Left and the old Right is not entirely surprising; as Gad Horowitz, amongst others, has pointed out, both streams of thought have at their core some form of collectivism. That is to say, the focus upon individualism in Canadian political thought is generally tempered by a recognition of the larger community (social, cultural, or economic) within which individuals find themselves. The social unit itself is essential to protect what is important about each person; thus, abstract discussions of individualism or individual rights without consideration of the nature of the polity are either misleading or simply irrelevant.

The complex relationship between Tory and progressive values is intriguing, and one of the great debates in Canadian political thought is whether this dynamic forms the basis for most Canadian political thought. However, the expression of these values in political thought rarely manifests itself currently in the form of nationalism. This shift is part of a larger trend. In political science itself, the concept of "state sovereignty" is increasingly decried rather than defended. In contemporary political philosophy, the dominant issue is why liberal values, which are ostensibly "universal" values based upon the quality of human life per se, frequently end at state borders. In a sense, the logic of liberalism has itself contributed to the undermining of the state system whose raison d'être, particularly in the United States, was to protect and defend liberal values. In Canada, as we have seen, the role of the state was, originally, quite different.

The original purpose of the Canadian colonies was to contribute to Britain's political and economic interests, and Canadian policy, even after Confederation, was oriented to a defence of British interests and culture. The first commanding articulation of a convincingly Canadian sovereignty was perhaps outlined by Henri Bourassa, grandson of Louis-Joseph Papineau and founder of *Le Devoir*. Bourassa had a clear vision of a Canada shared equally by English and French cultures, and he castigated both parties quite emphatically for failing to work toward this partnership. His case against English Canadians was quite clear, and it was, on many counts, similar to that uttered by French-Canadian nationalists. English Canada was too obsequious and servile to British interests—and too negligent of French-Canadian ones. Canada was quick to send its young men to die in the Boer War—Britain's war—in 1899, and the same sentiment against Canadians dying in British or European wars fuelled the Conscription Crisis in 1917. Canada was willing to pay for a new navy, only to place it under British command. At the same time, Canada's immigration policy encouraged the settlement of "Galicians, Doukhobors, Scandinavians, Mormons, or Americans of all races," in addition to convicts from England, and restricted the settlement of both French Canadians and French-speaking Europeans. Because of subsidies granted by the Canadian government, Bourassa pointed out, it was cheaper for an immigrant to travel from the slums of Liverpool to Winnipeg than it was for "the hardy sons of Quebec" to travel to Manitoba.[15] But Bourassa's condemnation of "that class of English-speaking Canadians, in whom patriotism and devotion to the flag, the Constitution and the Crown, are swayed by racial bigotry and exclusiveness," was matched by his scolding of all French Canadians who did not stand up to English Canadian bigotry:

Above all, we fail in our duty to the British Crown and the noblest portion of the British people, who once thought us high-minded and strong enough, morally, to share with them in the work of national construction, and whom we are seemingly endeavouring to convince that we would rather fall back to the rank and station of well-fed slaves.[16]

The consequence of English Canadians' sycophancy to the British and neglect of the French Canadians was, Bourassa warned, the "moral Americanization" of Anglo-Canadians. To a generation of Canadians raised on the assumption of the superiority of British morals, this threat was dire indeed. Yet while Bourassa appealed to the preservation of British values against the rising tide of consumerism, the "loud and intolerant patriotism," and the "worship of gold" that typified American society, his articulation of Canada was very much a partnership of equals, who could not only respect the uniqueness of the other but benefit from it. This vision stands quite clearly against the continentalism of Goldwin Smith, who, contemporaneously, argued that the very impossibility of Canada as a nation rested in its lack of cultural homogeneity.

Bourassa's depiction of American depravity was not completely unfair, given that it coincided with the worst excesses of industrial capitalism in the United States at the end of the nineteenth century. The political influence of the American "robber barons" coincided with the development of corrupt political machines like Tammany Hall, and the fraternity of Canadian business no doubt appeared quite gentlemanlike and civilized in comparison. However, the contrast between circumspect Canadian society in the 1950s, still largely rural, and postwar American society, with its productive capacity lighting the fire of modern consumerism, must have been even greater. Radio and television technology facilitated the development of American popular culture, which found a receptive audience in Canada. The political elites in Canada played down the impact of such lowbrow culture: two royal commissions (the Massey Commission in 1951 and the Fowler Commission in 1957) observed that "it was indeed fortunate that the minimal educational value of American mass entertainment meant that there was really no need to compete."[17] When the full impact of American postwar culture hit Canada, there was no substantial Canadian (or even British) alternative available, and Canadian intelligentsia looked on with dismay as generations of young Canadians uncritically absorbed American offerings.

The articulation of contemporary Canadian nationalism was, at first, a discussion of cultural difference. However, the most notable declaration of the importance of a distinct Canadian culture, George Grant's *Lament for a Nation*, was in fact a critique not only of American society but also of modernity per se. The impossibility of conservatism, as Grant famously wrote, was the impossibility of Canada. The United States was built upon the edifice of both freedom and technology, and liberal ideology thus reconciled the political power of the elites with the "titillation of the jaded tastes of the masses."[18] Within this reconciliation of power for the elites and moral permissiveness for the masses, the only purpose of life is consumption, and liberals demand the freedom to choose the form of consumption that they prefer. The political influence of each citizen is strictly circumscribed, as all real power is held by corporate interests; but individuals can still have a say in the kinds of items they buy. The liberal outlook tells us that, "if one cannot be sure about the answer to the most important questions," one should leave the task of answering up to each individual. Of course, the individual may be too distracted by the cornucopia of consumer goods to answer at all. In Grant's view, this moral laissez-faire can only lead to a complete failure to care about fundamental moral issues. Thus, he argues, leaving such important issues to individual choice is wrong. In the face of moral uncertainty, one should accept that "tradition is the best basis for the practical life." We may make the wrong moral choices, but we will at least have a rich social community in which moral choices actually *matter.*

Interestingly, two decades after Grant's threnody was published, American political philosophy itself began to echo many of these same concerns. A group of political theorists, including Alasdair MacIntyre, Michael Sandel, and Michael Waltzer (frequently, although not accurately, referred to as "communitarians"), began to challenge some of the assumptions of contemporary American liberal thought. These criticisms had a great deal of resonance in late twentieth-century America, but, unlike in Canada, no well-defined non-liberal tradition existed in the United States to which one could turn. The choice, as MacIntyre wrote, was to become either an Aristotelian or a Nietzschean, and few Americans likely found either option greatly attractive.[19]

In spite of George Grant's lament, many tenacious Canadians argued that Canadian culture was not doomed to follow in lockstep with that of the United States and that Canadian distinctiveness could be preserved *if* like-minded Canadians could maintain decision-making control over their society. The issue was thus not a *moral* one; the desire of Canadians to maintain a more communal outlook in their policy choices would not inevitably deteriorate as long as they had the political ability to support this option. The problem was that American corporations had interests that conflicted with this world view; and the threat to the Canadian way of life was thus in the ability of American multinationals to limit Canadians' political choices through corporate control of the Canadian economy.

In 1968, the concern over cultural dependence was eclipsed by a focus upon economic dependence, with the release of the Watkins Report, detailing foreign (but predominantly American) direct investment in the Canadian economy. Two years later, Kari Levitt published *Silent Surrender: The Multinational Corporation in Canada*, which provided an analytical explanation of the trend toward foreign ownership. This trend was, again, part of a larger, global one; André Gunder Frank, for example, had published the first major work in dependency theory, *Capitalism and Underdevelopment in Latin America*, in 1967. The concept of a resource-dependent economy fit well with the tradition of Canadian political economy developed earlier in the century by Harold Innis, who had pointed out the relationship between "metropolis" and "periphery" within Canadian economic development. According to the Canadian Left, Canada was dependent upon the interests of American capitalism for its economic development, and, left-wing theorists argued, where the interests of Canada and the United States diverged, the latter would prevail as long as Canada remained dependent upon American capital to develop its productive capacity.

Thus began an interesting strategic alliance between radical Marxists and old-school conservatives. Staunch Tories had never complained about the use of state policy to shape national institutions, and they no doubt viewed the Liberal government's stance on economic regulation as the more palatable of the Liberals' policy

measures.[20] The socialists and left-liberals, for their part, were scorn-
ful of the Tories' emphasis upon tradition, morality, and hierarchy,
but it was no worse than the vapid consumerism of American culture,
and it did focus discussion upon social well-being. During the early
1970s, the Liberal government established various agencies (including the Canadian Development Agency, the Foreign Investment
Review Agency, and Petro-Canada) as part of a "third option," which
would enhance state control of Canadian assets, permit economic
diversification away from resources, and establish alternative markets
to balance its trade dependency upon the United States.

What happened to the debate over Canadian sovereignty? The
issue of economic nationalism remained heated until the late 1980s,
when other issues displaced it. The fevered debates over whether
to sign a Free Trade Agreement with the United States coincided
with a rising tide of global neo-liberalism. While popular opinion
on the issue was evenly split, the state of Canada's unimpressive
economy seemed to suggest that the price of autarchy might be
material hardship; this thought, in turn, implied that the best strategy to sustain economic growth was to risk the vagaries of the global
marketplace. The demise of increasing numbers of Marxist states
reinforced neo-liberalism as an international doctrine, and, if
Canadians chose not to view the market as a benign instrument,
fewer still viewed it as inherently destructive to national interests.

However, if globalization enhanced the influence of neo-liberalism, it also shifted the focus of the Left. In the 1990s, the clearest
division between the Left and Right in Canada, as elsewhere, was
on the issue of international trade reform and, specifically, on the
effects of a proposed Multilateral Agreement on Investment (MAI).
Left-wing groups across the globe found themselves united in the
argument that this measure would give large corporations too much
power over national governments. When the attempt to develop a
MAI was aborted in 1998, the Left took Marxism back to its roots
and increasingly considered the struggle against capital as one that
had to be waged at the global, not national, level. In Canada, this
increasingly global focus has led to another split within the Left
between traditional left-nationalists and those who, like Paul Kellogg,
have argued that supporting Canadian capitalists to fend off
American ones does little to further socialist goals. Kellogg points
out that, with resources making up only six per cent of GDP, Canada

can hardly be considered "resource dependent," and, if Canadian manufacturing is experiencing a decline, the same is true in "every single advanced economy in the world," including that of the United States. "The facts," concludes Kellogg, "simply do not support any aspect of the Canadian left-nationalist dependency school."[21]

Discussions of Canadian identity have, like the Left, become less tied to economic nationalism. Unlike the Left, however, Canadian political thought has increasingly looked inward at largely domestic issues (albeit those which have global resonance). In doing so, it has in fact developed an identifiable "core" that incorporates all of the historical streams noted previously. Canadian identity, at the turn of the millennium, has become closely tied to issues of social well-being (most manifestly, health care but also child care, gun control, single-sex marriage, and the medical use of marijuana), and economic sovereignty has been displaced by issues of "micro-identity," which emphasize the role of ethnic units over national states. Jacksonian liberalism, with its strong emphasis upon equal political rights and liberal universalism, has had a major impact in Canada (sometimes ironically, as in the establishment of same-sex rights). Canada has also chosen to follow the tradition of nineteenth-century British liberalism in its attempt to use the state to construct an environment that can secure the well-being of its citizens (through, for example, health care and, tentatively, child care). At the same time, the Tory respect for culture and tradition is echoed in the current emphasis upon minority rights. From these three traditions, a Canadian perspective has emerged, one that articulates an account of individualism based upon the recognition of equality, order, and context.

NOTES

[1] For more on conservative thought in America, see, for example, Shadia Drury, *Leo Strauss and the American Right* (New York: St Martin's Press, 1997).

[2] Goldwin Smith, "The political destiny of Canada," in H.D. Forbes, *Canadian Political Thought* (Toronto: Oxford University Press, 1985) 115-33.

[3] "The American Apologists," *The History of Economic Thought Website*, Department of Economics, New School for Social Research, New York, 16 Sept. 2005 <http://cepa.newschool.edu/het/schools/apologist.htm>. For a wider discussion of the development of the Manchester School, see the article "The Manchester School" from this website at <http://cepa.newschool.edu/het/schools/manchester.htm>.

[4] S.D. Clark, "Canadian community and the American continental system," *The Developing Canadian Community*, 2nd ed. (Toronto: University of Toronto Press, 1968) 192.

5 Clark, "Canada and the American value system," *The Developing Canadian Community* 237.

6 Barry Cooper, "Western political consciousness," *Political Thought in Canada,* ed. Stephen Brooks (Toronto: Irwin, 1984) 215.

7 C.B. Macpherson, *Democracy in Alberta: Social Credit and the Party System* (Toronto: University of Toronto Press, 1953) 35.

8 Macpherson, *Democracy in Alberta* 220.

9 Cooper, "Western political consciousness" 231.

10 See, for example, John Richards and Larry Pratt, *Prairie Capitalism: Power and Influence in the New West* (Toronto: McClelland and Stewart, 1979).

11 Nelson Wiseman, "Provincial political cultures," *Provinces: Canadian Provincial Politics,* ed. Chris Dunn (Peterborough: Broadview Press, 1996) 54.

12 Michael Adams, *Fire and Ice: The United States, Canada, and the Myth of Converging Values* (Toronto: Penguin Canada, 2003) 84.

13 To illustrate this, Adams places the Prairie provinces very closely to the Atlantic provinces in his regional schema of several socio-cultural values: see Adams, *Fire and Ice* 81.

14 Adams, *Fire and Ice* 72, 75.

15 Henri Bourassa, "The spectre of annexation," 1912, *The Development of Political Thought in Canada: An Anthology,* ed. Katherine Fierlbeck (Peterborough, ON: Broadview Press, 2005) 38.

16 Henri Bourassa, *National Disintegration: Responsibility of the French Canadians* (Montreal: Le Devoir, 1912) 36.

17 See J.M. Bumstead, "Canada and American culture in the 1950s", *Interpreting Canada's Past,* ed. J.M. Bumstead (Toronto: Oxford University Press, 1986) 406. The Fowler Commission, writes Bumstead, noted that "Some American television programmes are no doubt filled with either too much commercialism, too much violence or other undesirable features. For such programmes, the good taste of Canadian viewers, their different and independent judgement could be safely relied upon to deal adequately."

18 George Grant, *Lament for a Nation* (Ottawa: Carleton University Press, 1982) 59–60.

19 Alasdair MacIntyre, *After Virtue* (Notre Dame: University of Notre Dame Press, 1984). More recent scholarship, however, argues that the tradition of civic republicanism in early America was clearly distinct from that of Lockean liberalism.

20 See, for example, Gad Horowitz's discussion of the role of "red Tories" in *Canadian Labour in Politics* (Toronto: University of Toronto Press, 1968).

21 Paul Kellogg, "After left nationalism: the future of the Canadian political economy," *Marxism* 2 (2004): 21–31.

PART
2

SOCIAL JUSTICE

UNDERSTANDING THE
5 CULTURE OF SOCIAL JUSTICE

Canadian political thought is the product of numerous intellectual currents, including the British Tory tradition, constitutional liberalism, American market liberalism, and French-Canadian nationalism. These streams of thought have produced two dominant trends in contemporary Canadian political thought. The first is social justice, and the fact that Canadian attitudes on this principle have diverged (and arguably continue to diverge) so clearly from those of Canada's American neighbour at a time when global convergence is assumed makes this trend worth examining in some detail. The second, the recognition and accommodation of cultural practices, is a more recent phenomenon. It is an intellectually powerful account, but whether it has surpassed the traditional liberal view of how to accommodate ethnic minorities remains unclear.

This chapter looks at the reasons that "social justice" has become an identifiable characteristic of Canadian political thought and policy vis-à-vis the United States. Part of the reason is evident from the discussion in Chapter Three: social justice is the legacy of British traditions, including both Toryism and welfare liberalism. However, this claim itself has been the subject of a long intellectual discussion, and the first part of this chapter will look at an element of this discussion, the "fragment theory" debate, in some detail. The second part of this chapter looks at another possible explanation for these ideals of social justice: the particular manifestation of religious organization in Canada.

THE FRAGMENT THEORY

The concept of a "fragment theory" was articulated in 1955 by Louis Hartz in a study entitled *The Liberal Tradition in America.*[1] Hartz, an American scholar, argued that socialism was not able to take root in American society because the United States was, since its inception, a clear outgrowth of a "liberal fragment" of European immigration. In order to take root, socialism, because of its collectivist nature, required a tradition of organic collectivism (common in formerly feudal societies). Because the United States did not have a tradition of feudalism, it was not amenable to the development of left-wing thought. Nine years later, Hartz edited a collection of comparative studies that applied this "fragment theory" to a number of different states.[2] Hartz identified three kinds of fragments: feudal (such as Latin America and Quebec), liberal/bourgeois (United States, English Canada, Dutch South Africa), and radical (Australia, British South Africa).[3] A "fragment" of European society was "extracted" from the parent society and implanted into a colony, and these fragments, rather than following the trajectory of their parent state, became fixed at their point of origin.

According to Hartz and Kenneth McRae (who had contributed a study on Canada in the comparative volume), Canada, excepting French Canada, was very much like the United States in that it was predominantly a liberal society. Hartz accepted that Canada did have a little streak of Tory culture in its composition, but he stated that the influence of this "tory touch" was negligible for the purpose of his analysis. Hartz did not know how much of an impact this throwaway comment would have on generations of Canadian students. It was precisely upon the issue of how important this Tory touch was to Canadian society that Horowitz based his 1966 article "Conservatism, liberalism, and socialism in Canada: an interpretation." Horowitz argued that, far from being insignificant, this Tory streak was crucial in differentiating Canada from the United States:

> The most important un-American characteristics of English Canada, all related to the presence of toryism, are (a) the presence of tory ideology in the founding of English Canada by the Loyalists, and its continuing influence on English-Canadian political culture; (b) the persistent power of whiggery or right-wing liberalism in Canada (the Family Compacts) as contrasted with the rapid and easy victory of liberal democracy (Jefferson, Jackson) in the United States; (c) the ambivalent centrist character of left-wing liberalism in Canada as contrasted with the unambiguously leftist position of left-wing liberalism in the United States; (d) the presence of an influential and

legitimate socialist movement in English Canada as contrasted with the illegitimacy and early death of American socialism; (e) the failure of English-Canadian liberalism to develop into the one true myth, the nationalist cult, and the parallel failure to exclude toryism and socialism as "un-Canadian"; in other words, the legitimacy of ideological diversity in English Canada.[4]

From a very broad comparative perspective, stated Horowitz, these Tory streaks may well seem insignificant. However, from "the point of view of one who is interested in understanding English Canada not merely as a bourgeois fragment, but as a unique bourgeois fragment, the imperfections are significant."[5]

H.D. Forbes is probably correct that Horowitz's objective in his analysis was not simply to elucidate the distinction between Canadian and American political cultures but also to make the case that a home-grown socialist movement in Canada was both a natural outgrowth of Canadian culture and a phenomenon that differentiated Canada quite clearly from the United States.[6] Forbes is also probably right in his argument that the popular resonance of Horowitz's article for generations of Canadians has not been because of the analytical strength of the fragment theory itself (Forbes effectively outlines a number of analytical weaknesses in Hartz's theory) nor because of Horowitz's account of a natural niche for Canadian socialism. Rather, the fragment theory was popular, he argues, because Horowitz demonstrated persuasively that Canadians' political culture was, *contra* Hartz, quite distinct from that of the United States. Horowitz, Forbes allows, does explain that Canadian conservatism *has* had "a different tone and different intellectual structure from American conservatism; it has played a more legitimate and perhaps more influential role in public life."[7] Nevertheless, argues Forbes, the argument that "toryism in Canada accounts for the existence of socialism in Canada" does not clearly follow. Rather, he suggests, socialism in Canada has become more popular because, regardless of its origins, it allows Canadians to distinguish themselves from Americans.[8]

In an intriguing twist, however, it is not the Left that has been able to capitalize on Canada's putatively Tory past, but those who argue for the recognition of differential rights for cultural minorities. The current movement toward the preservation of the ethnic identity of groups and away from the universal protection of uniform individual rights has fit very nicely with the concept of a "corporate-organic-collectivist" tradition in Canada. There is, of course, no little irony in this, given that the original Tory tradition in Canada was very much a result of a conquering imperialist power whose cultural objectives, where they were articulated at all, were primarily related to the diffusion of Enlightenment principles, including rationalism, universalism, and individualism.

What, then, can be said about the Hartz-Horowitz thesis at forty? The first observation must be that there is still little agreement about the significance of the "tory touch." As Ajzenstat argues, the men of the Château Clique and Family Compact were not Tories in the strict sense, as they certainly did not put the common good before individual interest. They were simply oligarchs. And the Fathers of Confederation were not Tories either: their focus was upon the establishment of a liberal democracy, not a feudal society.[9] Yet it is more difficult to dismiss the less forceful claim that Canadians are slightly more Tory in their liberal-democratic affiliation, that they accept the values and principles of both liberalism and democracy, but in a more moderate and less individualistic way than the Americans. Nonetheless, even if Hartz was wrong and Horowitz was right about the significance of the "tory touch," the implications of this Tory streak are quite different than what Horowitz had in mind.

The second observation one can make about the Hartz-Horowitz thesis is that most scholars now dismiss the idea of a temporal progression of ideological principles implicit in this account. Both Hartz and Horowitz, according to Forbes, accepted the Hegelian-inspired Marxist argument that "feudalism gives rise to the capitalist bourgeoisie which eventually destroys its own foundations" and evolves into socialism.[10] A great deal of historical scholarship has since established that nineteenth-century Canada was, in fact, characterized by an ongoing debate between those holding quite distinct ideological principles. This book traces a number of separate ideological strands in the formation of Canadian intellectual traditions, but these streams are neither exclusive nor rigidly bound. The canvas of early Canadian political thought was quite colourful; it was not simply characterized by a chiaroscuro of "Tory" versus "liberal" thought, but dappled by a range of ideas focusing on democratic principles, constitutionalism, private property rights, the role of the Church, and so on.

Acknowledging the diverse shades of Canadian political thought leads to the third contemporary criticism of the Hartz-Horowitz thesis, which is that it completely neglects ideological trends that are not easily arranged into "feudal" or "liberal" categories. Critics of the fragment theory argue that the categories employed by Hartz were both sloppy and arbitrary. (Forbes uses the idea of "feudalism" as an example.) More recently, scholars such as Gordon T. Stewart have introduced the category of "civic republicanism" (also sometimes referred to as "local communalism") as a major influence in the formation of both American and Canadian political thought.[11] According to this account, civic republicanism was liberal in its support for democracy and its rejection of authoritarian governance, but it also stressed collectivist values and rejected rampant individualism or subservience to market forces. Ajzenstat and Smith argue that civic republicanism had its genesis in the anti-Enlightenment but democratic philosophy of Jean-Jacques Rousseau:

> Envisaging a one-class society of small property owners, farmers, and independent craftsmen, civic republicanism supposes that those representing the community institutions of government will articulate a sense of the common good and an idea of civic virtue to which all members of the polity adhere.[12]

These accounts have admittedly expanded the theoretical depth of the tradition of Canadian political thought, and have shown that, rather than consisting of a predictable set of dominant ideological sentiments, Canada's intellectual past was nuanced and complex. But this complexity itself raises an epistemological problem. While it may be fascinating to think about these nuances—whether Egerton Ryerson was really a liberal, rather than a Tory; whether Canadian political figures were more concerned with classical virtues than with merely maintaining the prejudice of tradition; or whether participatory democrats were in fact demonstrably distinct from constitutional liberals—one risks fragmenting the history of Canadian political thought into an endless multitude of discrete "traditions." Pushed to the extreme, one can say that every political figure has been influenced in some way by one or another existing tradition. Conversely, one could also say that every thinker with something original to express is, by definition, unique. Thus, the question of how many significant "streams" of Canadian political thought exist is, to an extent, arbitrary and dependent upon one's evidence, and the evaluation of this evidence, while an academic's proper job, can be confusing and tedious to others.

Notwithstanding all this, the "hard fact," as Forbes acknowledged, was that the Left became stronger in Canada than in the United States, and the explanation of why this is so remains an interesting endeavour. Published almost forty years after Horowitz's article, Michael Adams's evaluation of polling data taken from both Canada and the United States upholds the claim that Canadians are simply more progressive in their political values than Americans are.[13] The "tory touch" (or possibly "civic republicanism") is, to some degree, a likely explanation. But are there other factors? Elizabeth Mancke, for example, sensibly points out that the existence of the "strong state" tradition in Canada can be traced to the institutional configurations made by the British government (frequently in reaction to the "centrifugal developments" arising in Britain's American colonies).[14] These administrative decisions were political and strategic, and they were based upon the interests of Empire rather than on philosophical or ideological concepts. Still, they resulted in a distinct political framework for Canada, and one that proved to be quite conducive to the development of progressive legislation in the twentieth century. A second variable, and one that we should examine more closely, is the role of religion in the development of Canada's political culture.

THE ROLE OF RELIGION

In the twenty-first century, Canada seems very much a secular society. Only 30 per cent of Canadians consider themselves to be devout, so policy-makers heed their political constituents much more closely than religious authorities when legislating new laws and programs. This secularism makes Canada distinct from the United States; over two-thirds of Americans consider themselves to be regular church-goers, and American politicians are very mindful of religious lobby groups. This distinction is especially interesting in view of the fact that the United States was established upon the principle of a clear division between Church and State, while Canada formally recognizes a monarch who is also the head of the Church of England. However, if the Church in contemporary Canada plays little direct role in influencing the current direction of policy-making, its historical legacy in Canadian political thought is considerable. The first reason underlying the import of religion in Canadian politics is precisely that the political elites and the traditional social establishment in Canada were irretrievably connected with the Anglican church (also known as the Church of England). Early Anglican organizations in Canada could appeal for support (usually in the form of funding and manpower) from the colonial authorities. The colonial authorities, for their part, clearly recognized that the spread of Anglican doctrine (facing the challenge of both the Roman Catholic Church and, more worrisomely, other Protestant factions) could reinforce loyalty to the British imperial government.

It is instructive to remember, however, that while the Anglican church remains the formal religious institution of England, the United Church, in the words of S.D. Clark, has become "the fullest expression" of the identification of a religious movement with the national community of Canada.[15] This is an important point. The character of modern American politics is infused with the principles of fundamentalist evangelical movements. (Even George Bush, during the 2000 election campaign, is reputed to have said that "on the issue of evolution, the verdict is still out on how God created the earth."[16]) This evangelical fundamentalism has led politics to the right of the political spectrum in the United States. Remarkably, a form of Protestant evangelical faith also became, as Clark noted, the closest thing that Canada has had to a national church. Yet the United Church, like its earlier Methodist incarnation, has imparted a more *radical* character to Canadian politics. It is worth investigating this paradox in more detail.

How did Methodism come to play such a prominent role in the formation of Canadian political values? Methodism began in 1739 in Britain as a splinter movement established by disaffected Anglicans. The direct cause was a dispute over doctrinal matters; but, as Elie Halévy argued in his classic 1913 analysis of the movement, its immense popularity occurred because it coincided with the Industrial Revolution, which left tremendous social upheaval in its wake. "The despair of the working class," writes Halévy, "was the raw material to which Methodist doctrine and discipline gave a shape."[17] The notable feature of the Methodist movement for the next two centuries was its ambivalent political nature, both radical and conservative. Methodism became in England very much a social movement, propelling its well-to-do members to lives of philanthropy and political reform. Doctrinal squabbles were pushed aside in order to focus upon the abolition of slavery, the atrocious working conditions of urban labourers, and the reform of both criminal law and penal organization. By the early nineteenth century, the development of socialism and Chartism in Britain increased political tensions between classes. "The fellowship in Methodism protected the Church against the worst dangers of class divisions," and, as E.P. Taylor observed, "its theology helped, in a peculiarly favorable age, to develop a strong individualistic self-consciousness, which led men to assert their rights in politics."[18] At the same time, however, early Methodism was itself hardly a democratic movement: its internal organization and the attitudes of its proponents were noticeably hierarchical and conservative.

This ambivalence, unsurprisingly, resulted in the fragmentation of the Methodist movement, and two dominant factions resulted, each embodying one of the coexisting opposites. The Wesleyan sect, on one side, "championed authority in Church and State, and were Tories." The Free Methodists, on the other side, "raised the standard of liberty, and were avowed Liberals."[19] Both forms of Methodism were quite prevalent in the settlement of Britain's North American colonies. Following the War of Independence, however, the Free Methodists, along with other forms of "Dissenting" Protestantism, became the dominant religious force in the United States; the Wesleyans, with their strong historical ties to the Church of England, became more prominent in Canada, where they nonetheless had to compete with the well-endowed, carefully organized Anglican church, which represented the early colonial power elites. The War of 1812 effectively institutionalized the split between the more extreme Protestant sects in the United States, which began to develop in response to the libertarian politics and the "materialism and social fragmentation associated with the rise of urban industrialization," and the more conservative forms practiced in Canada.[20] It was the War of 1812, argues historian J.L. Little, that convinced the radical American missionaries that their limited resources would be put to better use "in their own country's rapidly expanding west-

CHAPTER 5: Understanding the Culture of Social Justice | 95

ern frontier" than in Canada's more established Eastern Townships, which were already dominated by more conservative Protestant denominations. Even though the fundamentalist sects (such as Millerism) did exist in Canada in the early nineteenth century, they received little support there and eventually disappeared.

It should be noted, however, that American fundamentalist groups had better success in the Canadian West in the early twentieth century. The Prairie provinces, and especially Alberta, experienced a great deal of American immigration in the late 1800s and early 1900s, and the disproportionately American population (particularly in Alberta) facilitated the transfer of more extreme religious beliefs. Still, the relative weakness of radical fundamentalism in Canada does not explain why Methodism would contribute to a stronger sense of social justice in Canadian political thought. Indeed, Canadians being generally more conservative in their religious views than Americans would seem to suggest just the opposite.[21] However, the Methodist Church was able to find its own niche in Canada—and one that incorporated concern for social justice— partially because of the Anglican church's grip on the early colonial elite. While Methodism in Britain had developed in response to the devastating forces of urban industrialization, Methodism in Canada was able to take advantage of the harshness of rural homesteading in culturally heterogeneous communities. The Methodist Church's "saddle-bag preachers had bravely served where few other clergy would venture and had brought an emotionally satisfying, fervent religion to an immigrant society deeply in need of spiritual comfort and social regeneration, and to a demoralized native population on the verge of extinction."[22] Most evangelical sects found greater success in the hinterland and in "marginal urban areas" in the early nineteenth century, and, in these areas, the evangelical movements in the West were able to compete more easily with the established Anglican church.

But the "radical" quality of Canadian Methodism rested, rather paradoxically, upon the very material success of early Canadian businessmen. A significant number of wealthy Canadian entrepreneurs in the late nineteenth and early twentieth century belonged to the Methodist Church, and Methodist doctrine encouraged this wealth to be used for spiritual purposes. Methodism was especially clear about the virtue of hard work and material reward:

The growing temporal success of church members might be a legitimate sign of spiritual progress since it reflected at least a partial
victory of untamed nature. Making and saving money also encouraged diligence, hard work, and discipline and stimulated frugality
and benevolence."[23]

The rise of prominent Methodist businessmen such as Hart
Massey, Timothy Eaton, James Lougheed, and Robert Simpson also
coincided with the rise of the Social Gospel Movement, which
became extremely influential between the 1890s and the 1930s.
Methodist doctrine held that "[s]ince the Bible taught that the rich
must help the poor, spending money properly was a religious test
and an act of worship."[24] This principle was expanded by the Social
Gospel Movement (a broad affiliation of like-minded progressive
evangelicals) to hold that the duty of the rich to the poor included
the active attempt to achieve broader political and economic
reforms on behalf of the less well-off. Many of Canada's early political progressives began their careers as religious activists. J.S.
Woodsworth, William Irvine, and Eugene Forsey, who became instrumental in establishing the Co-operative Commonwealth Federation
in 1932, were all previously quite active in the Social Gospel
Movement. By World War I, the Social Gospel had become "a
primary informing principle of social reform."[25] Many of the early
objectives of the movement reflected the conservative orientation
of the traditional religious movements (temperance, social purity,
eugenics, and sabbath observance); however, by the end of World
War I, the goals of the Social Gospel Movement focused more
squarely upon the expansion of universal suffrage, economic redis-
tribution, and bureaucratic reform.

In 1925, the Methodist Church amalgamated with the
Presbyterian and Congregationalist churches to form the United
Church of Canada. By the 1920s, the Social Gospel Movement itself
was experiencing a palpable decline, but the centralization of the
Canadian evangelical tradition into a single institution concentrated the social and political influence of the movement. As historian Neil Semple argues,

The United Church has helped to convince Canadians that they share
the fundamental obligation to advance social justice, human rights,

and moral progress. The success of the church can perhaps be best measured by the degree to which the state has accepted this prescribed role and implemented many of the social-welfare programs originally advocated by the Methodist and United Churches.[26]

The Social Gospel was an active force in the United States as well. But in Canada, the ideological force of the Social Gospel was facilitated politically by a state that was traditionally accepted as a vehicle for the promotion of social morality and even religious organization. In both English- and French-speaking regions of Canada, there was much less resistance to the use of the state to secure social welfare than in the United States, where state involvement in social legislation was viewed with a great deal of suspicion and resentment. It was the Social Gospel Movement, according to some, that was largely responsible for Canadians' willingness to embrace both the construction of an encompassing new welfare state after World War II and the country's role as a peacekeeping nation.[27]

One should nonetheless keep in mind that the social progressivism of the Methodist Church, and even of the early United Church, was in keeping with the progressivism of the day and age: in other words, proponents of fairer labour laws for factory workers could easily espouse the obvious cultural supremacy of English-speaking Protestantism, and those arguing for prison reform might see no reason to object to the forced sterilization of "idiots and cretins." On some issues, this tension was readily apparent: the male leadership of the early Social Gospel Movement, for example, was very slow to accept the principle of women's suffrage. Loyalty to Great Britain was historically a marker of Canadian identity, and, because early evangelical movements in Canada were quickly associated with American republicanism, they were obliged to be clear about their loyalist credentials. Protestant movements were relatively similar in their assumption of British cultural supremacy (with the consequent attitudes of racism that this engendered), and, even in 1947, S.D. Clark could say, in one of his treatises on religion in Canada, that "Canadians have not felt sufficiently secure in their national attachments to cultivate an attitude of tolerance."[28] Yet the United Church's roots in the Social Gospel have clearly shaped this church into one of the more culturally sensitive and socially progressive religious institutions in the country, with one of its modern mandates being "to improve ethnic relations and to dissipate racial tensions through tolerance and mutual respect."[29] Interestingly, however, vestiges of the tension between moral conservatism and social progressivism remain and can be seen in such curious phenomena as, on the one hand, the United Church's acceptance of same-sex marriage and, on the other hand, its (successful) lobby for sabbath observance in Nova Scotia, which continues to ban Sunday shopping.

There are two questions that seem to define the discussion about the Left in Canada. First, "why has the Left done so well in Canada?" Second, "why has the Left done so poorly in Canada?" Both questions are difficult to answer definitively. The first query, as we have seen, usually arises when Canada is compared to the United States. The answer to it usually involves some discussion of Canada's "corporate-organic-collective" tradition of Toryism; of Canada's heritage of colonial administration, which emphasized a strong role for the state; of the role of the United Church as a dominant religious institution in Canada; and of other explanations (such as the ability of some American administrations, and especially that of Roosevelt, to co-opt the agenda of the Left more effectively at a crucial historical point). Those who contrast Canada to European states tend to ask the second question. Despite establishing itself as a political force early in the twentieth century, the Left has never formed a national government, and its successes at the provincial level, while consistent over time, do not seem to translate to support at the federal level. How have Canadian thinkers interpreted radical ideas to a Canadian idiom, and how have their ideas influenced radical politics in Canada? The following chapter looks at the way in which intellectuals outside the liberal-Tory tradition have understood radical principles, and have reconceived them as Canadian ones.

NOTES

1 Louis Hartz, *The Liberal Tradition in America* (New York: Harcourt Brace, 1955).
2 Louis Hartz, ed., *The Founding of New Societies* (New York: Harcourt Brace, 1964).
3 The fragment theory is still alive and well. Forty years on, for example, Edward Grabb and James Curtis have employed a form of the fragment theory, arguing that the American South would constitute a feudal society, largely due to its acceptance of the institution of slavery. See *Regions Apart: The Four Societies of Canada and the United States* (Toronto: Oxford University Press, 2005). Also, H.D. Forbes and Nelson Wiseman have published a lively debate about the extent to which French Canada can and

ought to be considered a "feudal" society and about how it fits into the broader Hartzian claim concerning the relationship between feudal fragments and socialist movements. See H.D. Forbes, "Hartz-Horowitz at twenty: nationalism, toryism and socialism in Canada and the United States," *Canadian Journal of Political Science* 20.2 (June 1987): 287–315; Nelson Wiseman, "A note on 'Hartz-Horowitz at twenty': the case of French Canada," *Canadian Journal of Political Science* 21.4 (December 1988): 795–806; and H.D. Forbes, "Rejoinder," *Canadian Journal of Political Science* 21.4 (December 1988): 807–11.

4 Gad Horowitz, "Conservatism, liberalism, and socialism in Canada: an interpreta-tion," 1966, *The Development of Political Thought in Canada: An Anthology*, ed. Katherine Fierlbeck (Peterborough, ON: Broadview Press, 2005) 213.

5 Horowitz, "Conservatism, liberalism" 213.

6 Forbes, "Hartz-Horowitz at twenty" 308–12.

7 Forbes, "Hartz-Horowitz at twenty" 304.

8 Forbes, "Hartz-Horowitz at twenty" 308–12. In support of this observation, see Paul Kellogg's article outlining the relationship between nationalists and socialists in Canada: "After Left Nationalism: The Future of Canadian Political Economy," *Marxism* 2 (2004): 21–31.

9 Janet Ajzenstat, *The Once and Future Democracy: An Essay in Political Thought* (Montreal and Kingston: McGill-Queen's University Press, 2003) 6.

10 Forbes, "Hartz-Horowitz at twenty" 290.

11 Gordon T. Stewart, *The Origins of Canadian Politics: A Comparative Approach* (Vancouver: UBC Press, 1986).

12 Janet Ajzenstat and Peter J. Smith, "Liberal-republicanism: the revisionist picture of Canada's founding," *Canada's Origins: Liberal, Tory, or Republican?* (Ottawa: Carleton University Press, 1995) 8.

13 Michael Adams, *Fire and Ice: The United States, Canada, and the Myth of Converging Values* (Toronto: Penguin Canada, 2003).

14 Elizabeth Mancke, "Early modern imperial governance and the origins of Canadian political culture," *The Canadian Journal of Political Science* 32.1 (March 1999): 3–20.

15 S.D. Clark, "Religious organization and the rise of the Canadian nation," *The Developing Canadian Community*, 2nd ed. (1962; Toronto: University of Toronto Press, 1968) 115–30.

16 Quoted by *New York Times* syndicated columnist Maureen Dowd, 3 February 2005.

17 Elie Halévy, *The Birth of Methodism in England*, trans. Bernard Semmel (1913; Chicago: University of Chicago Press, 1971) 70.

18 E.P. Taylor, *Methodism and Politics, 1791–1851* (New York: Russell and Russell, 1975) 150.

19 Taylor, *Methodism and Politics* 202. Taylor recounts how Methodist liberals would defend their political affiliation, saying that "if I am a Chartist, my Bible has made me so" (206).

20 J.L. Little, *Borderland Religion: The Emergence of an English-Canadian Identity, 1792–1852* (Toronto: University of Toronto Press, 2004) 143.

21 This is precisely the argument of S.D. Clark's 1945 essay "The religious sect in Canadian politics." See Clark, *The Developing Canadian Community*, 2nd ed. (1962; Toronto: University of Toronto Press, 1968) 131–46. "While it is true that the evan-gelical churches have at times lent support to the cause of political radicalism, it is questionable whether such support has been nearly as significant as supposed in revealing their political thinking" (131).

22 Neil Semple, *The Lord's Dominion: The History of Canadian Methodism* (Montreal and Kingston: McGill-Queen's University Press, 1996) 180.

23 Semple, *The Lord's Dominion* 339.

24 Semple, *The Lord's Dominion* 340.

[25] A. Richard Allen, "Social Gospel," *The Canadian Encyclopedia,* 2005, Historica Foundation of Canada, 20 Sept. 2005 <http://www.thecanadianencyclopedia.com/index.cfm?PgNm=TCE&Articled=A0007522>.

[26] Semple, *The Lord's Dominion* 447.

[27] A. Richard Allen, "Social Gospel," *The Canadian Encyclopedia.*

[28] Clark, "The religious influence in Canadian society," *The Developing Canadian Community* 172.

[29] Semple, *The Lord's Dominion* 443.

CHAPTER 6

RADICAL POLITICAL THOUGHT

Canada's radical tradition has been "radical," to a large extent, in the very particular sense of acknowledging the "inherent, essential, and fundamental" character of its Tory heritage against the powerful tide of liberal individualism. The Tory tradition, as we have discussed, is often seen as the reason that socialist thought has been more prevalent in Canada than in the United States. Yet much socialist thought, despite its rhetoric of a common good, was built upon the foundation of scientific rationalism that has, since the Enlightenment, also steadied the edifice of liberal political thought. While the stream of socialist (and social democratic) thought common in twentieth-century European states has not been absent in Canada, the fact that Canadian socialism was based largely on agrarian populism as well as industrialism has had an enormous influence upon the way in which Canadian theorists have thought about socialism. The mechanics of the relationship between wage-labourers and capitalists has been more muted, and a broader focus upon material egalitarianism and the common good (and the use of the state to achieve this) has been more pronounced. Industrial strategies may have been the focus of radical intellectuals in southern Ontario, but the opaque idea of "collective" action is what has facilitated the success of social democratic movements at the provincial level. This form of Canadian radicalism was increasingly viewed as quaintly anachronistic in the late twentieth century, but the decline of a manufacturing base for most Western democracies has, ironically, meant that socialist movements tied too closely to industrial organization may fare far worse than those based upon the more romantic idea of a common good that informed agrarian collectivism.

THE LEFT

The Left in Canada faces at least four distinct challenges. Two of these are definitively Canadian problems; the other two confront all modern social democratic movements. The first challenge is Canada's lack of a substantial industrial base and its historical dependence upon agrarian populism. This challenge is compounded, of course, by the regional structure of Canada's economy: the bulk of heavy manufacturing occurs in a corridor stretching across southern Ontario through to Montreal, while western and eastern provinces depend more substantially upon agricultural production and resource extraction. Traditionally, workers in the industrial sector had an interest in minimizing the entry of goods from other countries, while those in the agricultural and natural resource sectors sought to export their goods to the denser American markets. (This difference, for example, lay beneath the politics of the 1911 Reciprocity Treaty). Moreover, workers in the industrial sector are generally highly organized, well represented, and have little vested interest (beyond employment) in their jobs, while agricultural and natural resource-based workers are poorly organized, less represented, and (in agriculture) often own the property on which they labour. Consequently, the socialism of southern Ontario is quite different than that of, say, Saskatchewan or British Columbia; and the first challenge of socialism in Canada has always been to find a correspondence of interests that will appeal to both types of groups without alienating either.

The second challenge is the relationship between the Left and the *concept* of the state. In Canada, the willingness of the Left to harness the state to achieve particular aims has been one reason that it has, in fact, made substantial legislative achievements. Canada, being a federal state, however, has also meant that the Left has had to ask "*which* state?" when focusing upon policy strategy. A strong national state presence has generally been viewed as a means of achieving social democratic goals (and executing them equitably across the country), but the strong centralism of the Left has also been fiercely contested by regional actors across the political spectrum (most notably in Quebec).

The third challenge is not confined to Canada and involves a question that has been debated for as long as democratic socialism has existed: to what extent ought the Left to try to attract broad electoral support by moderating its policies and to what extent should it attempt to hold fast to its less popular principles?[1] The fourth can also be framed as a question, one that now confounds all social democratic movements in the twenty-first century: how ought the Left to think about social democracy in a much more globalized world, with so much wealth being generated through various patterns of international trade? By tracing the historical development of leftist political thought in Canada, this chapter considers these four challenges to Canadian socialism.

The political thought of the Left in Canada originated in two quite distinct phenomena. The first was agrarian populism, which was, in its genesis, neither particularly socialist nor manifestly Canadian. Throughout the 1800s, small farmers' organizations evolved, and they had straightforward aims: to meet the specific commercial, educational, and social needs of the rural populations. By the late 1800s, however, farmers began to realize that the concentration of both economic interests and voting populations in southern Ontario meant that this region was the beneficiary of much government policy. The tariff on American goods favoured the manufacturers, but prevented Canadian farmers from easily exporting their goods to the large American market. The railroads were monopolized by central Canadian corporations, which were able to maintain high freight charges for farmers wishing to transport their goods to market. Financial institutions, most of which were based in Ontario and Quebec, profited from the failures of farmers during times of drought or recession. Farmers saw that the most efficient solution to this lack of control over their lives, and livelihoods, was political organization.

The first large agrarian movements were branches of successful American farmers' organizations. The two largest were "the Grange" and "the Patrons of Industry," both of which established themselves in Canada in the 1870s. By the beginning of the twentieth century, most agricultural regions had their own autochthonous organizations: in Ontario, the Dominion Grange and Farmers' Association was created in 1907 while, on the Prairies, the Grain Growers' Association was the dominant representative. The success of these movements in representing the interests of farmers was most obvious in their ability to convince Laurier's government to lower the tariff in 1911. The Reciprocity Agreement, however, infuriated the established manufacturing interests, and Laurier's government was defeated the same year. The tariff remained. It was compounded by a major depression from 1912 to 1915, causing farmers to become even more radical and politically astute. In 1914, Ontario farmers established two separate but affiliated organizations: the United Farmers' Organization (UFO), which successfully formed the provincial government a short time later, and the United Farmers' Cooperative Company (UFCC), which was responsible for the commercial activities of the farmers. In Manitoba and Saskatchewan, the Liberal governments were essentially agrarian parties while, in Alberta, the United Farmers of Alberta (UFA) formed its own political party.

The second dimension of early radical thought in Canada was derived from British and American socialist movements. The American Socialist Labor Party espoused a clear Marxist vision, and British immigrants brought with them the traditions of Owenism, Chartism, Fabianism, and Christian Socialism. By 1903, the most dominant socialist organization was the Socialist Party of Canada, which was overwhelmingly proletarian and Marxist in character. The intellectual aspect of socialist thought for the first decades of the twentieth century was notably lacking, especially in contrast to both the United States and Great Britain: "the main work of implanting the socialist idea in Canada during this formative period," writes Norman Penner, "was done by these self-educated people, all of them members of the working class."[2]

Internationally, socialism was already fractured by doctrinal divisions, most emphatically on the issue of whether the Left ought to work within the system of capitalist democracy or to destroy and replace capitalism completely. Interestingly, Canadian socialism, at this point, was clearly in the latter camp; the more moderate Fabians and Labourites were not well represented within the Socialist Party of Canada.[3] The tension between hard-liners and moderates eventually resulted in the formation of the Social Democratic Party of Canada in 1911. By 1921, however, both the Socialist Party of Canada and the Social Democratic Party in Canada had been eclipsed:

The Communist Party had emerged with a new brand of Marxism based on the Russian experience and the teachings of Lenin. The

Ontario section of the Canadian Labour Party, the Independent
Labour Party in Manitoba, Saskatchewan, and Alberta and the
Federated Labor Party of B.C. became the repositories of the British
labor-socialist idea, but were not ready for some time to coalesce into
a nationwide political entity.4

One of the greatest drawbacks of the Canadian Left at this point,
notes Penner, was its doctrinaire quality, "its inability to use Marxism
as an analytical tool to better understand the specificities of the
political, social, and economic environment of Canada."5 Of such
specificities, the farmers' movements had a great deal, although,
as C.B. Macpherson argues, the agrarian populists simply did not
have a clear idea of the root causes of their exploitation. The two
movements had a common cause, and they also had complementary strengths. Therefore, it is not surprising that there should have
been some cooperative action between them; nor is it surprising
that their differences, in most cases, caused them to diverge enor-
mously in the following decades.

At first, the primary undertaking of both farmer's organizations
and workers' associations was consciousness-raising. Both movements stressed to their members that they comprised a *class* and that
their class interests would be furthered if they organized themselves
to these ends. Both farmers and workers saw themselves as exploited
by the same groups: the urban financial elites and the manufacturing interests of Toronto and Montreal. Agricultural producers and
industrial workers, however, perceived the nature of their exploitation differently. The farmers resented the political power that the
manufacturers held over government policy and the economic power
the financiers held over vital economic institutions while the workers fought the poor wages and lack of regulation over working conditions. The farmers hated the railroads for their control over
transportation while railway workers condemned their primitive
working conditions, low wages, and lack of legal safeguards.
Nonetheless, both groups viewed the results in the same way: the
exploited class suffered, and the moneyed elites prospered.

To a certain extent, too, the perceived solutions were similar for
both groups. The Non-Partisan League, an American agrarian
movement that quickly made its way to western Canada, advocated
government ownership of agricultural services and facilities (such

as elevators and processing plants). Both rural agrarian and urban industrial workers rebelled against the vestiges of Tory autocracy and privilege and saw the advantages of a class-based system of representation. The "group government" espoused by Henry Wise Wood (where agrarian and industrial workers would each be represented in government by their own political arm) was noticeably similar to the principles of guild socialism. Saskatchewan had even formed a "Farmer-Labour" Party in 1925; in Ontario, the leader of the UFO, E.C. Drury, had clear labour leanings; and, even in Alberta, the UFA was quite ready to cooperate strategically with labour.[6]

Nonetheless, real substantive differences remained between the agrarian and socialist movements. The former were quite emphatic about their populist character, even though C.B. Macpherson has argued that the particular manifestation of "quasi-party" politics in Alberta led to a centralization of power in both the UFA and the Social Credit governments as the membership became less active and "decisions came increasingly to be made by a small group at the top."[7] Still, the articulation of democracy was important to the agrarian movement's self-identity, and it differed quite considerably from the centralization of control espoused by the Communist Party. In 1919, for example, the Western Labour Conference unanimously adopted a resolution in support of the new idea of "proletarian dictatorship," which was seen "as being absolute and efficient for the transformation of capitalist private property to communal wealth."[8]

This divide over how much to centralize power in the quest for social justice also underscored a second significant incompatibility between the two groups: the farmers were largely the owners of private property while many socialists stated their intent to abolish private property. Agricultural producers desperately needed access to the American market for their produce while an open border jeopardized the security of Canadian manufacturers and threatened unemployment for their workers. One of the first clear indications of the limited support one group could expect from the other was seen during the Winnipeg General Strike of 1919. Lasting forty-two days, the strike was a major revolt against the abysmal wages and working conditions endured by labourers in a rapidly growing but poorly regulated municipality. A number of sympathy strikes occurred across Canada, but this spurred fears that the country was about to experience a "nation-wide revolutionary plot."

Public awareness of the successful Russian Revolution two years earlier did not calm these anxieties. Farmers, too, were largely unsympathetic to the strikers' cause; the strike had diminished their capacity to market their goods, "and they considered demands for a six-hour day as sheer laziness bordering on the absurd."9 Prairie populists had as little patience for Big Labour as they did for Big Business while the Communist Party insisted that "poor farmers" had to be made aware of their exploitation by "rich farmers."

This mix of radical ideologies led to decades of shifting alliances between interesting bedfellows. By the middle of the 1920s, the farmers' political party, the Progressives (which received the second largest share of the federal vote in 1921) had disintegrated; many returned to the Liberal fold, while the more radical agrarians, led by the "Ginger Group," combined with independent labour politicians, progressive academics, and many social democrats to form the Co-operative Commonwealth Federation in 1933. Its founding document, the Regina Manifesto, clearly stated the party's intent to reject revolutionary violence and to seek the eradication of capitalism through constitutional and parliamentary means. While there was some implicit recognition that the CCF could represent the interests of the Left in parliament so that the Communist Party could concentrate upon "extra-parliamentary strategies" (such as protests), the two parties fought bitterly over union support. The Communist Party "found it easier to advocate unity with the Liberals than with the CCF," and indeed King's reform liberalism effectively stalled public support for the CCF by implementing many of the welfare programmes for which J.S. Woodsworth had long been advocating.10 The CCF, however, made a determined effort to hold on to the farmers' political support. The greatest threat to the agrarian base of the CCF (and to that of its successor, the NDP) was its success is wooing union support away from the Communists in the 1940s. A final link of note is the curious genesis of Social Credit, generally considered to be fairly far to the right on the political spectrum. It was, in fact, Independent Labour MP William Irvine (later one of the founders of the CCF) who had introduced the ideas of C.H. Douglas to Canada.11

The most notable characteristic of the Canadian Left, then, is that, in contrast to the situation in the United States, it exists in any significant form at all. The Left's continuing role in Canada has arguably been due to its success at securing a sizeable non-industrial base. The second characteristic is that, as in most European liberal democracies, leftist radicalism takes the form of a movement willing to work within both democratic structures and the confines of capitalism. The Canadian Left's period of moderation was punctuated by the 1944 CCF convention, in which Frank Scott, David Lewis, and M.J. Coldwell argued for a more temperate socialism; the 1956 Winnipeg Declaration, which emphasized the need for the reform of capitalism (in place of its eradication); and the formation of the New Democratic Party in 1961. The Communist Party, which had allied itself ideologically with Leninism, strategically with the Communist International, and politically with the USSR, found itself increasingly marginalized as the political reputation of the Soviet system foundered in the west after World War II. The creation of the NDP, with its formal relationship to Canadian unions, reinforced the moderates' position of dominance over the revolutionary Left.

The third feature of the Left in Canada is its economic nationalism. Woodsworth himself was a Canadian nationalist, although his target was Britain, and his aim was the patriation and revision of the BNA Act. The League for Social Reconstruction (an early think tank of the CCF) published two documents—*Social Planning for Canada* and *Who Owns Canada?*—that noted the conflict between the interests of Canadians and those of foreign investors.[12] Interestingly, it was precisely on the issue of foreign economic control that the Canadian Communist Party had its one significant conflict with the Communist International. The leader of the Canadian Communist Party, Tim Buck, took Lenin's call to examine "the particularities of each nation" to heart, so, in 1930, he observed that Canada experienced economic domination by both Britain and the United States. This observation did not sit well with the official position of the Comintern, which was that Canada was itself "a fully independent capitalist state."[13] Buck retracted his position after suitable encouragement from the Comintern, although he was, in retrospect, more than vindicated by the surge of economic nationalism within the New Democratic Party from the 1960s on.

The late 1960s was a period of radical protest in most Western democracies. The curious aspect of the Canadian wave of radical protest is that it sought to strengthen the Canadian state, rather than dismantle it. In 1969, a breakaway movement of young radicals from the established New Democratic Party released a statement, subsequently known as the "Waffle Manifesto," which argued that a socialist Canada needed to address the penetration of American corporate capital in the Canadian economy.[14] The Waffle movement only lasted three years, but it had an enormous impact upon both public sentiment and federal Liberal policies. For over a decade, public debate focused on the need to strengthen "Canadian interests" against those of American multinationals, and the Liberal administration of Pierre Trudeau did implement a number of measures to address American multinational investment. Conservatives claimed these policies were dangerous; social democrats argued that they were toothless. By the late 1980s, trade patterns, industrial performance, and neo-liberal sentiment undermined support for "Canadianization of the economy," but even those on the Left began to realize that economic nationalism was becoming little more than a contest between Canadian corporate capitalists and American corporate capitalists.

The era of economic nationalism in Canada does underscore the close relationship between the Canadian Left and the Canadian state. This closeness would seem at first glance to belie the impact of agrarian populism upon the Canadian Left. Yet we must remember that the farmers' organizations, like most political movements, were not ideal types: they were primarily pragmatic responses to pressing political problems. While most farmer-politicians expressed a deep dislike for an intrusive state, they nonetheless supported state ownership or control of key facilities such as grain elevators, flour mills, and produce processing plants. They adopted the philosophy of social credit, which had been introduced to Canada by the Left, and they agitated for clear regulation and control (and sometimes ownership) of financial institutions by the state. The farmers' ambivalent relationship to the state is reflected in modern politics, where agrarian interests insist that the state play an active role when circumstances demand it.

One must also recognize that most Marxist theory throughout the 1970s and 1980s focused on the particular relationship between "capital" and "the state" in most Western democracies. By the 1950s, it had become fairly clear that the capitalist system, despite various burps and hiccups, was relatively stable and showed no signs of imminent demise. To explain the longevity of capitalism, Marxist theorists began to examine the role of the state in perpetuating the dominance of the bourgeoisie. Marxist state theory discussed the way in which the state could maintain the "ideological hegemony" of capitalism. Based on the ideas of Antonio Gramsci, Louis Althusser argued that the presence of "ideological state apparatuses" worked as a subtler and more effective complement to repressive state methods to reinforce the strength of capital vis-à-vis labour.[15] Nicos Poulantzas and Ralph Miliband debated the nuances of the relationship between state and capital: what were the causal pathways that allowed capital to ensure conditions necessary for its survival? Were capitalists able to hold politicians on a short leash (using, for example, the risk of capital flight), or did elected officials themselves generally pursue these strategies with little direct motivation from business (largely because a prosperous economic climate meant a greater likelihood of re-election)?[16]

With the advent of global recession in the early 1970s, Marxist state theory took on a new dimension. This became known as "crisis theory," and fit the political climate of the times quite well. The best known of these works is perhaps James O'Connor's *Fiscal Crisis of the State*, published in 1973.[17] It argued that the capitalist democratic state had two major functions: to help "reproduce the conditions" of capital expansion (through tax cuts, appropriate labour legislation, the provision of infrastructure, and so on) and to maintain a stable and efficient workforce (through the provision of education, social welfare, and some legislative protection for the workforce). As industrialism became more sophisticated, the skill level of workers increased as well; the workforce had to be well-educated, healthy, and willing to work. As industrial production increasingly depended on complex technologies and computerization, jobs required a higher level of intellectual engagement as well as technological skills. This was the reason that capitalist states often had the best social welfare systems. As long as the capitalist state could perform both of its functions (i.e., encouraging capital expansion and maintaining a relatively contented workforce), crisis theorists described capitalism as stable. However, they argued, there was an inherent contradiction in these two state functions. When the economic climate was strong, states could offer both benefits to capital (such as tax breaks) and to citizen-workers (unemployment benefits, health care, education, and so on). But when the economy hit a major obstacle, the state could not meet the contradictory demands placed on it. Economic crisis would lead to political crisis, and the inability of the state to deal with either would lead to an ideological crisis, which, optimistically, would allow everyone to see the true nature of capitalism and to be more receptive to alternative systems.

Marxist state theory was perhaps the dominant form of Marxist political thought throughout the 1970s and 1980s, and it had much resonance in Canada given the very close historical relationship in Canada between capital and the state. A great deal of Marxist theory at this time analysed the relationship between various aspects of the economy and various levels and departments of the Canadian state. The best example of this is perhaps Leo Panitch's *The Canadian State: Political Economy and Political Power*.[18] By the late 1980s, however, the Left was to experience yet another major shift.

Partly in response to the lengthy dominance in Marxist theory of scholarship emphasizing the state, young scholars began to focus on the specifically *non*-state actors that had been long neglected by the Left. The new intellectual trend for the Left was Social Movement Theory, an intellectual approach that attempted to move beyond "simple economic reductionism" to explain the nature of modern collective action. Researchers became interested in issues such as culture and identity, and they tried to fit these variables into a more complex understanding of social activism. In fact, Laclau and Mouffe, Habermas, and Offe had discussed many of these issues within a more Marxist framework in the 1980s.[19] Later theorists, however, moved even further away from orthodox Marxist analysis. By the 1990s, radical political thought had to a large extent displaced Marxism in favour of a new trend: postmodernism.

OTHER FORMS OF RADICALISM

The impact of postmodernism upon Marxist thought in Canada was quite considerable partially because postmodernism addressed many of the sources of unease that radical intellectuals had with orthodox socialism. There were at least three major concerns. The first was the neglect of a rich conception of democracy. Marxism's focus upon Lenin's "dictatorship of the proletariat" historically, and upon the role of the state more recently, left a great lacuna in the area of civil society. Certainly Marx had a clear, if poorly articulated, idea of what "democracy" was to be, and it definitely was not liberal democracy, with its protection of private property rights. But by the end of the twentieth century a form of intellectual fatigue had set in. Although a great deal of discussion had concentrated on how capitalism was to be defeated, undermined, or controlled, considerably less attention was given to what ought to be put in its place. Marxist thought seemed at a dead end. The authoritarianism of the Soviet system was, in any case, poor advertising for all accounts of political centralization.

The second criticism of Marxist thought was related, and it focused upon the extremely rationalist approach that characterized much of modern Marxism. This criticism was probably somewhat unfair, as, throughout the twentieth century, popular objections to Marxism had been related to its "utopianism" and its failure to consider some of the more obvious consequences of Marxist doctrine logically and systematically.[20] However, even as liberal philosophy began to be criticized for its one-dimensionality, its lack of a more nuanced account of what it means to be "human," and its methodological insistence upon an achievable Truth, much Marxist theory attempted to become even more scientifically rigorous.

The third deficiency of Marxism was that it was concentrating on economic variables and formal political institutions to the exclusion of other factors that many believed to be rather important. The impact of feminist theory was pivotal here, both from a political and an epistemological perspective.[21] Women's groups focusing upon political issues have existed in Canada since the late 1800s. The earliest organizations were either missionary or temperance societies, such as the Women's Christian Temperance Union, and were middle-class movements based on the assumption of women's moral superiority. Later women's movements, such as the Voice of Women and the National Action Committee on the Status of Women, were also considered "bourgeois" organizations whose simple mandate was to achieve equal status with males. By the 1970s, the women's movement began to fracture into liberal feminism (which focused upon legislative equality), socialist feminism (which focused upon the needs of women in the industrial labour force), and radical feminism (which held that patriarchal oppression did not necessarily involve issues of class or economic structures). Radical feminists began to question the way that power and knowledge were constructed, and they argued that socialist feminists often reproduced the patterns of oppression established by bourgeois liberals. By the 1990s, feminists became more interested in how reality was "constructed" in such a way that patriarchy was able to survive the challenges mounted by both liberals and socialists. This epistemological insight was a major theme of late twentieth-century thought, and it formed the basis of much postmodern discussion.

As well as feminism, issues of race and the environment affected Marxist political thought in the late twentieth century. Racial issues had played an ambivalent role in radical American thought from the late 1960s, but their presence in Canada was far more muted. Despite Canada's relatively large population of visible minorities, the issue of race in political thought became prominent only when intellectuals from outside western democracies began to examine the legacy of colonialism.[22] The dearth of theoretical literature did not mean that the politics of race was either unimportant or non-existent in Canada. First Nations groups, in particular, gained a much higher profile in Canada than in the United States. They achieved prominence in the formal political arena (becoming participants in federal-provincial negotiations), in the courts (especially over land claims), and in radical political confrontations (such as the standoff at Oka). It was, however, not upon Marxist theory but rather upon liberal rights theory that the intellectual foundation for aboriginal groups began to coalesce.

Another movement in Canada that had an uneasy intellectual relationship with the Left was the ecological movement. Although a number of eco-activist groups such as Greenpeace and the Sierra Club had organized around various controversial Canadian issues, it was largely the profile of prominent scientist David Suzuki that brought middle-class respectability to (and broader public support for) environmental issues. While the NDP was a natural home for ecological movements because of a shared interest in the ability of government to control corporate activity, this tenuous partnership between green movements and the Left obscured a divisive conflict. Most obviously, the traditional support of the Canadian Left came from the industrial workers and the agrarian commodity producers, both of whom had little direct interest in preserving the natural state of the land. More abstractly, the traditional Marxist affirmation of both industrial society's triumph over nature and the vital role of political conflict sat poorly with the ideas of respect for nature and cooperative collectivism that informed the political values of the ecological movements.

What all three contemporary intellectual movements—feminism, anti-racism, and eco-activism—did have in common was a deep scepticism of the primacy of economic factors, of the benign nature of a strong state, and even of rationalist conceptions of knowledge themselves. One Canadian intellectual who perceived very early on the limitations of the Left for radical political movements was George Woodcock. Like many young political activists in the 1930s, Woodcock was involved in, and very influenced by, the anarchists' role in the Spanish civil war. Anarchism itself, of course, has had a long and complex relationship with the Left, beginning with Proudhon and Bakunin. Like Marx, anarchists believe that individual freedom can only be achieved in the absence of oppressive state institutions. Most anarchists also believe that the monopolization of economic resources also hinders the development of free individuals. After World War II, when liberal and socialist perspectives dominated much ideological discourse, anarchism was dismissed as being obsolete and utopian. However, the fundamental insights of anarchist thought—that some of the most valuable qualities of being human are destroyed by an over-institutionalized society—became clearly relevant even as liberal ideology celebrated its victory over state socialism in the late 1980s.

Despite the exhilaration felt by those on both sides of the Iron Curtain over the liberalization of the Soviet Union after 1989, a significant proportion of political theory in the West was, at the same time, addressing the feeling many had that something important was nonetheless missing from liberal democracy. Both "communitarian"-oriented philosophy and "civil society"-oriented political science (such as Robert Putnam's essay "Bowling Alone") acknowledged that informal or organic social organization was being undermined by contemporary ways of living, and that individuals were suffering because of it.[23] These were, in fact, the analytical observations made by anarchists decades earlier. The solution presented by anarchists was not simply the abolition of state and bureaucratic structures but, as Woodcock argues, the need for a greater decen-tralization of power throughout modern polities.[24]

Nevertheless, anarchism lacked the epistemological depth that postmodernism, at its best, was able to exhibit. It also lacked a crucial component of the analysis of the individual that postmodernism was able to offer: this was the idea of "the construction of human identity." Most new social movements throughout the nineties and beyond did, in fact, recognize the principle, neglected by decades of liberal thought, that collective action and communal life were essential for the achievement of group objectives. The generations that espoused these ideas, however, were also the products of decades of liberal ideology. They refused to jettison the idea of "the individual" (and individual rights), attempting rather to reconcile the individual with the society that produced her. What makes contemporary movements so fascinatingly complex, and what divorced them from the Left as a mainstream movement, was the argument that collective action and social groupings were impor-tant, not simply for the groups they protected, but for the multi-dimensional well-being of the *individuals* within these groups.

NOTES

[1] See, for example, Adam Przeworski and John Sprague, *Paper Stones: A History of Electoral Socialism* (Chicago: University of Chicago Press, 1986).

[2] Norman Penner, *The Canadian Left: A Critical Analysis* (Scarborough: Prentice Hall Canada, 1977) 43.

[3] Penner, *The Canadian Left* 45.

[4] Penner, *The Canadian Left* 68.

[5] Penner, *The Canadian Left* 75.

[6] "The U.F.A.," writes historian W.L. Morton, "could claim labour support in every federal electoral district in which a U.F.A. candidate was running." See *The Progressive Party in Canada* (Toronto: University of Toronto Press, 1950) 243.

[7] C.B. Macpherson, *Democracy in Alberta: Social Credit and the Party System* (Toronto: University of Toronto Press, 1953) 218.

[8] Quoted in Penner, *The Canadian Left* 65.

[9] Walter D. Young, *Democracy and Discontent: Progressivism, Socialism, and Social Credit in the Canadian West* (Toronto: McGraw-Hill Ryerson, 1969) 22.

[10] Penner, *The Canadian Left* 169.

[11] Admittedly, the original concept of government control over the creation of credit was not incompatible with socialism. Irvine, in adopting this monetary theory, "did not switch from socialism to social credit, because he did not see the two as incompatible. He merely added a method of socializing credit to the particular style of socialism he had already espoused, which was akin to, but not identical with, guild socialism." See Anthony Mardiros, *William Irvine: The Life of a Prairie Radical* (Toronto: James Lorimer, 1979) 146.

[12] See Penner, *The Canadian Left* 197–212.

[13] Penner, *The Canadian Left* 92–97.

[14] For a more detailed account of the Waffle movement, see John Bullen, "The Ontario Waffle and the struggle for an independent socialist Canada: conflict within the NDP," *Interpreting Canada's Past: After Confederation*, ed. J.M. Bumstead (Toronto: Oxford University Press, 1986) 430–52.

[15] Louis Althusser, "Ideology and ideological state apparatuses," *"Lenin and Philosophy" and Other Essays* (New York: Monthly Review Press, 1971) 127–86.

[16] Nicos Poulantzas, "The problem of the capitalist state," *New Left Review* 1.58 (Nov.-Dec. 1969): 67–78; Ralph Miliband, "The capitalist state: reply to N. Poulantzas," *New Left Review* 1.59 (Jan.-Feb. 1970): 55–60.

[17] James O'Connor, *Fiscal Crisis of the State* (New York: St Martin's Press, 1973). See also Claus Offe, *The Contradictions of the Welfare State*, ed. John Keane (Cambridge, MA: MIT Press, 1984).

[18] Leo Panitch, ed., *The Canadian State: Political Economy and Political Power* (Toronto: University of Toronto Press, 1977).

[19] See, for example, Ernesto Laclau and Chantal Mouffe, *Hegemony and Socialist Strategy: Towards a Radical Democratic Politics* (London: Verso, 1985); Jurgen Habermas, *Lifeworld and System*, trans. T. McCarthy (London: Polity Press, 1987) Vol. 2 of *The Theory of Communicative Action: A Critique of Functionalist Reason*; and Offe, *The Contradictions of the Welfare State*. The first major work on social movement theory was perhaps Charles Tilly's *From Mobilization to Revolution* (New York: McGraw-Hill, 1978); but a good compilation of more mature social movement theory is Aldon D. Morris and Carol McClurg Mueller, eds., *Frontiers in Social Movement Theory* (New Haven: Yale University Press, 1992).

[20] See, for example, John Dunn, *The Politics of Socialism* (Cambridge: Cambridge University Press, 1984) and A.B. Atkinson, *The Economics of Inequality* (Oxford: Clarendon Press, 1983).

[21] An excellent history of the women's movement in Canada is written by Alison Prentice, Paula Boure, Gail Cuthbert Brandt, Beth Light, Wendy Mitchinson, and Naomi Black, *Canadian Women: A History*, 2nd ed. (Toronto: Harcourt Brace Canada, 1996).

[22] See, for example, Edward Said, *Orientalism* (New York: Pantheon Books, 1978) and *Culture and Imperialism* (New York: Knopf, 1993). The first "post-colonial" theorist, however, was Franz Fanon, who published *Damnées de la Terre* (*The Wretched of the Earth*) in 1963 (New York: Grove Press).

[23] Putnam's essay was expanded in the book *Bowling Alone: The Collapse and Revival of American Community* (New York: Simon and Schuster, 2000).

[24] George Woodcock, "Reflections on decentralism," *The Anarchist Reader*, ed. George Woodcock (Glasgow: Fontana Paperbacks, 1977) 326–32.

PART
3

CULTURE AND
ACCOMMODATION

CHAPTER 7

FRENCH-CANADIAN
NATIONALISM

The relationship between French Canada and English Canada has arguably been the most defining characteristic of the country's politics. In true Hegelian fashion, the development of much Canadian political thought has been the result of the contest between currents of thought emanating from English and French Canada. Many of the intellectual streams that developed within Quebec have focused on the attempt to preserve the region's language and religion and, occasionally, other cultural traits. This does not imply that French Canadian thought is monolithic: the nationalist stream itself is comprised of many different threads. The two most obvious of these are conservative (or ultramontane) nationalism and left nationalism, and both of these threads can again be dissected into discrete accounts. Also, while discussing streams of nationalist political thought in Quebec, one must never forget the powerful articulations of modern liberalism, many of which can be found in the journal *Cité Libre*, that came from the province at the same time.

There is some debate whether liberal political currents in Quebec can be described as "nationalist" at all, as liberal thought is generally directed at establishing the rights and freedoms of individuals in *opposition* to the overarching claims of nation. Yet the liberal conception is in fact a clear vision of what modern Quebec society should be. It holds that a Quebec polity is dependent upon the individual decisions of its citizens rather than upon an idea that is carefully and deliberately constructed at the level of state policy. Whether individuals in Quebec are able to nurture and shape a society that they find "meaningful" without the active use of government policy to protect cultural practices is, of course, the issue at the root of theories of collective right, which will be discussed in greater detail in the following chapter.

THE CHURCH IN LOWER CANADA

The political authority of New France after its founding in 1608 rested largely upon the Catholic Church. Champlain's New France was not founded as a settlement, but as an outpost designed to accommodate the fur trade. But settlement did eventually occur, and France established a formal colonial government in 1763. The Church in New France was able to maintain a remarkably substantial degree of power within the new civil government, and, as Claude Bélanger describes, "in the absence of a state, the Church became the state, if we understand the state's primary functions to be to regulate the life of individuals and to provide community services."[1] At the same time, the Gallican freedoms meant that the French state protected the Church from direct political intervention by the Vatican.*

Until recently, many have seen this period as one characterized by "clerical absolutism," with a powerful Catholic Church continuing a tradition based on feudal (or "seigneurial") patterns of authority. However, historians have more recently noted that the early settlers of New France had, during certain periods, much more freedom than previously supposed. Many of the "seigneurial" functions were performed by individuals who were themselves farmers or former farmers.[2] There was insufficient local economic development to permit a significant economic elite to emerge, and, like many early frontier settlements, the small size of the communities, and the hardships they endured, often blurred much of the rigid social stratification of the Old World. Moreover, by the early nineteenth century, the population boom in the settlements meant that "the population did not fall so clearly under the watchful eye of their priests."[3]

The most emphatic challenge to the authority of the Catholic Church came with the conquest of New France by Britain in 1760. Within three years of this conquest, Britain proclaimed that the Church of England would become the formal religious authority. It was, ironically enough, the increasing rebelliousness of the American colonies that re-established the presence of the Catholic Church in French-speaking settlements. By espousing a firm loyalty to British institutions in the face of American insurgency, the Catholic Church

---

* The Gallican freedoms comprised a doctrine of the ancient church of Gaul or France, and this doctrine asserted the freedom of the Roman Catholic Church, especially in France and her colonies, from the authority of the papacy.

in what was by now Lower Canada proved its usefulness in securing the allegiance of French-speaking subjects to Great Britain. By accepting and even propounding British authority, the Catholic Church secured its own independent existence. This independence would allow the Church to promote Catholicism within its own jurisdictions. The *Quebec Act* of 1774, which restored the authority of the Catholic Church as well as the practice of civil law, was seen as part of the quid pro quo negotiated by the Church with British authorities.

This accommodation was not merely an instance of political opportunism. The clericalism of the Catholic Church fit well with many of the Tory values of the British colonies, in opposition to many of the republican ideas that permeated the colonies from both Europe and the newly created United States. Monseigneur Joseph-Octave Plessis (later Bishop of Quebec) stressed this point in his 1799 sermon given during the commemoration of Nelson's victory over Napoleon. In the first place, he argued, the French Revolution had shown how depraved modern France had become. In the second place, Britain had not only offered refuge to those fleeing this carnage (and to the "descendants of the ancient heroes of France"), but had bravely entered into a war with "those who had usurped the sovereign authority in France."[4] Finally, in the third place, the moderation and respect for tradition evinced by the British was by far the most efficacious way of preserving the way of life for French-speaking Catholics.

Plessis was correct that British authorities had permitted a great degree of freedom for the French-speaking population to govern themselves as they saw fit. What increasingly restricted this freedom were the English-speaking colonists themselves, who bitterly complained about the freedoms granted the French-speaking settlements. The *Constitutional Act* of 1791, which created Upper and Lower Canada, diminished the voice of French-Canadians by creating political institutions that were more directly accountable to very vocal English-Canadian interests.

EARLY LIBERALISM IN FRENCH CANADA

Liberalism in nineteenth-century Quebec developed in response to two variables. The first was the conservative clericalism that still dominated the day-to-day lives of most French-speaking Canadians, and the second was frustration with the ostensibly "liberal" institutions that underscored the divisions between French- and English-speaking populations. The *Constitutional Act* had created elected legislative assemblies in both colonies, but these elected assemblies were subject to legislative and executive councils that were appointed by the governing power. For over three decades, the legislative assemblies in both colonies complained that their political voice was consistently being undermined by the councils, and, in Lower Canada, the obvious ethnic divisions between assembly and council compounded these institutional problems. "We have," argued Louis-Joseph Papineau in Lower Canada's Legislative Assembly, "only a misleading shadow of the English constitution; we have none of the advantages that ought to derive from it."5

Besides objecting to the institutional and political inequalities facing the French-speaking population in Lower Canada, liberals often criticized the influence exerted by Catholicism. By the beginning of the nineteenth century, a new professional elite in Lower Canada began to challenge the conservative authority of the Catholic Church. The young, well-educated francophones had several alternative political models to reflect upon, including the French revolutionary archetype (characterized by the Jacobins' emphasis on equality) and the American republican model (which stressed the political liberty of citizens). The Parti Canadien (known after 1826 as the Parti Patriote), which Papineau represented, contained both extreme radicals and more moderate reformers. Papineau's ideas well characterize the contradictions and complexities of the political thought of this era. Louis-Joseph Papineau considered himself a French-Canadian nationalist, and the nationalism of his day involved maintaining the institutions of clericalism and seigneurial property rights as well as the French language. But, especially after 1830, Papineau was also a strong democrat. He argued that democratic institutions did not preclude maintaining the underlying social structures, and he even asserted that the Church and the system of property ownership would ensure the stability of a democratic French-Canadian society. This outraged the more radical Patriotes, who pointed out that Papineau was himself a landholder with clearly vested interests.

But Papineau was very much a "liberal nationalist" in another interesting sense, as his nationalism was ethnically inclusive. What

Papineau and his followers desired was a constitutional reform that allowed the majority a real say in political decision making; the archetype of the agrarian habitant as the only true citizen of French Canada was not a part of the liberals' nationalism. This inclusiveness may well have been politically strategic as well as ideologically driven, as the Patriotes knew that they could count on the sizeable Irish Catholic community in their opposition to the Imperial colonial authority. The Party Patriote also included a number of English-Canadian members, whose support for the party was grounded in its espousal of democratic principles.

There is, unsurprisingly, a great deal of debate over the degree of "liberalism" in Lower Canada during this period. Nelson Wiseman, for example, is sceptical of Papineau's "never-too-lively" liberalism:

> Although at first sight Papineau appears to be a liberal, at a deeper level of analysis he remains *ancien, prérévolutionnaire, organiciste*. It is French Canada's feudal nationalism that clouds whatever liberalism it manages to throw up ... Papineau's liberalism and the later *rougisme* of the Institut Canadien need to be noted but not stressed.[6]

H.D. Forbes, however, responds that French Canada "had clearly acquired important elements of liberalism by the 1830s, as French-Canadian politicians had become very skilled in the rhetoric and devices of British liberal constitutionalism."[7]

Regardless of the force or the consistency of French-Canadian liberalism at this point, however, insurrections against the colonial authorities arose in both 1837 and 1838. Most historians agree that Papineau had lost control over the revolutionary Patriotes during the first insurrection, and that he was not even a direct participant in the second. Neither insurrection was successful, and in 1840, following the publication of Lord Durham's *Report on the Affairs of British North America*, the two colonies were united. French-Canadian nationalists of all stripes saw this unification as an utter failure because the result was seen to be eventual cultural assimilation—as Durham had recommended. At this point, liberalism as a political force in Lower Canada lost much of its force, and a conservative clerical form of nationalism became dominant once more.

Some threads of liberalism survived in Lower Canada nonetheless. A major venue for the expression of liberal ideas was the Institut

Canadien, founded in Montreal in 1844, which offered public lectures by leading French Canadian intellectuals. One of these figures was Étienne Parent, first a journalist and then a senior public servant, who recognized that the reality of unification meant that French-Canadian nationalism would require a new strategy. After 1840, then, French-Canadian liberals began to drift into two camps: one focusing upon the achievement of "responsible government" through parliamentary means, the other holding that the achievement of a society free from domination by either the British or the clergy was only possible in a politically independent nation.

Those in the latter camp were known as the Parti Rouges. Implacably opposed to Confederation, the Rouges were in the ideologically awkward position of arguing that a federal union would destroy "the French-Canadian way of life," even though they were themselves, for the most part, opposed to the Catholic clericalism that, during this period, still defined a great deal of the "French-Canadian way of life." In the end, the Rouges' self-imposed isolation marginalized them fatally. When political representatives met at Quebec City in 1864 to discuss the terms of Confederation, Canada East remained the only province without an opposition party represented at the table.[8] The Rouges lost a significant chance to influence what were to become the foundational principles of the new country.

In contrast to the extremism of the Rouges, the liberal-minded reformers argued that the *survivance* of French Canada could be best achieved within a nation governed by British parliamentary institutions. The problem, in the eyes of the reformers, was that these institutions were not grounded firmly *enough* on British principles. The most important of these was responsible government, in which the governor and his executive council were answerable to the elected Legislative Assembly. Were that in fact the case in Lower Canada, the French-speaking majority would have the ability to shape its own political decisions. "For myself," declared Louis-Hippolyte LaFontaine,

I do not hesitate to say that I am in favour of the English principle of responsible government. I see in its operation the only possible guarantee of a good, constitutional, and effective government. The inhabitants of a colony must have control over their own affairs. They must direct all their efforts toward this end; and, to achieve it, the colonial administration must be formed and controlled by and with the majority of the people's representatives.[9]

LaFontaine was emphatically successful in only a few years. Once in office, he repealed unpopular legislation, implemented electoral reforms, re-established the use of French as an official language, transferred the capital from Kingston to Montreal, secured the promotion of numerous French-speaking individuals to positions from which they had been previously excluded, and, most important, achieved responsible government in 1848. LaFontaine's success has defined the character of French-Canadian liberalism to this day. But hard-won political achievements frequently require compromise, and LaFontaine's victory, somewhat paradoxically, paved the way for greater clerical influence in political matters.

ULTRAMONTANISM

The alliance between the Catholic Church and LaFontaine's liberal reformers was advantageous for both parties. The Church quietly promoted the interests of the party to a still deeply religious electorate, and the party permitted the Church to retain its influence in areas such as education. "After 1846," notes Jacques Monet, "the clergy was to prove one of the great social forces working for the principle of responsible government."[10] The liberal principle of responsible government does not necessitate a progressive political platform, as a very conservative electorate will, unsurprisingly, favour a fairly conservative form of governance. Besides, because French-Canadian culture was tied so closely to the Catholic Church, it is understandable that a population concerned for its national survival would accept a strong role for the Church in day-to-day matters.

It is important to stress that the power of the clergy was not so much the result of disillusionment with liberalism as it was the consequence of its success. Although the radical liberals had suffered defeat both in their call for a separate nation and in their anti-clericalism, the liberal reformers who subsequently gained political control in Canada East cannot be considered either conservative or reactionary (except, perhaps, in direct comparison with

the radicals). The Church itself, however, was both, and ultramontanism, or the belief in papal infallibility, was the philosophical expression of these characteristics.

Like the ultramontanism of nineteenth-century Europe, the
"clerico-nationalist" elite in French Canada looked to the Vatican for
"inspiration and leadership" in combating the rise of Enlightenment
ideas. From the European ultramontane movement, French-Canadian
clergy derived "the same anti-modernist, undemocratic, intolerant,
and unenlightened views as were defined in the *Syllabus of Errors* by
Pope Pious IX."[11] Claude Bélanger has listed a number of characteristics of nineteenth-century ultramontanism in Quebec.[12] The most
common principle of all ultramontane belief was the precept that all
authority, even political, comes from the Pope in his role of God's
representative on earth. Ultramontanes considered the state to be
subordinate to the Church, and they held that the state was not to
limit either the scope or the degree of clerical influence. Concomitant
with this was political involvement by the Church in matters of the
day, largely to counter the influence of radical and liberal values
emanating from European states, America, and, occasionally, even
the Canadian colonies.

However, countering one pervasive idea associated with liberalism proved difficult for French-Canadian ultramontanes. This critical idea, developed during the French Revolution, was the concept
of a *state-based* nationalism. Because this nationalism was based upon
secular and rationalist principles, it was very much what the ultramontanes in Quebec wished to avoid. However, the "nationalist"
attempt to preserve the French-Canadian "way of life," based as this
life was upon conservative and religious principles, was exactly what
served the best interests of the Church. Thus, ultramontane "nationalism" took a very different form from that occurring in many
European states. This divergence underlines some of the interesting paradoxes of ultramontane thought in nineteenth-century
Quebec. It strongly supported responsible government, but opposed
the concept of democracy. It was a strong advocate of "nationalism," but decried the nationalist movement in Europe. And it was
a very politicized institution, yet it attempted to empty French-
Canadian nationalism of any real *political* content.

Nationalism, for the ultramontanes, was composed of Catholicism,
the French language, and various other social and cultural institutions,

including civil law, traditional families, the seigneurial system of landholding, and religious or classical educational institutions.[13] French-Canadian ultramontanism was, according to some, even "more orthodox than the Pope," and, like most nationalist movements, it had its own founding myths.[14] In 1958, Michel Brunet identified three pillars of French-Canadian thought.[15] The first of these was agrarianism. A good French Canadian was a devout habitant who lived off the land. Cities were the source of immorality and blasphemy (and, not coincidentally, the refuge of radical political movements). As McRoberts and Posgate point out, however, this "agrarian mythology" belies the fact that New France was established primarily as a trade outpost, not as an agricultural settlement, and that the length of time between the end of the fur trade and the commencement of industrialization meant that the practice of uninterrupted agrarian lifestyles was relatively short.[16] The second aspect of French-Canadian thought was anti-statism. This characteristic is not remarkable, as the Church itself had taken on many of the dominant functions of the state (including education, health care, and social assistance) and would find any expansion of state activity quite threatening. It may also partly explain the Church's historical animosity with the Left, especially considering the comfortable relationship elsewhere in Canada between religious movements and social democracy.

The third part of Brunet's typology, Messianism, is more ambiguous. It refers most explicitly to a nation under perpetual siege. There was certainly much evidence to support this view of the world. By the late 1800s, especially, French Canadians had seen the lack of concern given to the rights of francophones in Ontario, Manitoba, and New Brunswick, and the hanging of Louis Riel by the state graphically underscored the belief held by French Canadians that their way of life could only be protected within the geographical boundaries of a French-Canadian polity. The strategy of early ultramontane nationalism was to secure *survivance* within existing state structures. The republican values of America and France made it clear to the Church that French Canadians were better positioned within a relatively conservative Canada, which allowed them relative jurisdictional freedom. However, by the end of the 1800s, strong voices began to demand clear political autonomy for a French-Catholic state. The first systematic articulation of the need for an autonomous state was Jules-Paul Tardival's novel *Pour la patrie*, published in 1895. French-Canadian autonomy was not a dominant trend at this time, but other writers (especially the cleric and historian Lionel Groulx) did not discount the possibility of forming a separate state if that was what it took to preserve the character of French Canada.

The political thought of the ultramontane period, then, was most clearly defined by its nuanced apolitical quality, even though the control of the Church nonetheless had a definite impact upon the political character of Quebec. The ultramontanism of Quebec had rather more direct influence in theological and philosophical circles in the development of modern Thomism. Thomist philosophy was the strategy utilized by modern Catholic societies (and formally espoused by the Vatican in the late nineteenth century) as a response to the challenges of liberal epistemology and philosophy. Thomism, in effect, suggested a compromise between rationalism and religion in its acceptance of a circumscribed realm for the use of "reason." Where matters of faith conflicted with declarations of reason, however, the former took precedence. Still, even the compromise suggested by Thomism could not stem the scepticism that began to build in the middle of the twentieth century.

NEO-NATIONALISM AND SOCIAL RADICALISM

One might suggest that, compared to the highly reactionary nature of ultramontanism, any alternative form of political thought would appear to be radical. And, in fact, the simple development of a "technocratic" class is often seen as one of the factors leading to the Quiet Revolution of 1960. The sheer force of the province's conservatism, however, and the brutality with which politicians like Duplessis attempted to maintain traditional patterns of power, did, in fact, feed a strongly "radical" movement in the twentieth century.

If the intellectual elite of Quebec throughout the period of ultramontane dominance focused only upon issues of culture and religion, Quebec itself was changing nonetheless. As in the rest of Canada, the economy of Quebec underwent considerable structural transformation. In Quebec, however, industrialization had a particularly clear division of roles:

Entrepreneurs, markets, technology and capital came from outside Quebec, and were controlled by anglophones. Small trade and agriculture, which had been at the centre of the economic life of French Canadians, allowed for neither sufficient capital accumulation nor the formation of a financial and industrial bourgeoisie capable of taking advantage of the industrialization process. Quebec was able to contribute only its natural wealth and its cheap labour force.[17]

In addition to structural changes in the economy, the nature of Quebec's intelligentsia began to shift considerably. While the best and brightest had been trained for clerical roles throughout the nineteenth century, the very success of the Church at running many of the province's social and administrative institutions meant that the demand for qualified professionals in the early twentieth century increased beyond the capacity of the province to train them. Within a few decades, a critical mass of individuals educated outside the province coalesced; these individuals were frequently critical of the conservative hegemony. As Alain Gagnon notes, this cadre of intellectuals in the late 1940s and 1950s became the "intellectual vanguard of the anti-Duplessis social movement."[18] These individuals were largely trained within the social sciences, and at a time when Marxist methodology was increasingly prevalent.

The traumatic impact of the Depression and World War II had already begun to shake the complacency of many French Canadians, so, by the late 1940s, clerical conservatism began to come under greater scrutiny. Nevertheless, if social democracy defined much of the post-1960 nationalism in Quebec, it was not the relationship between classes that received the most attention but the relationship between Quebecois and the state. The social democracy of modern Quebec is a curious amalgam of ideas, and was perhaps more influenced by its Catholic collectivist past than by Marxist principles.

One aspect of nationalist thought after the Quiet Revolution, for example, was the use of the state to bolster both the Quebecois proletariat and the Quebecois bourgeoisie against the dominance of both foreign and English-Canadian capital. While many Marxists would want to employ the state to eliminate capitalism, social democrats in Quebec used it to *strengthen* French-Canadian capital. (This pattern, of course, also characterized the strategy of the Canadian Left in the 1970s and 1980s.) However, the neo-nationalism of twentieth-century Quebec was a complex hybrid that defies simple classification. The main driving force of change in Quebec was not the proletariat as much as the bourgeoisie, which was itself divided into at least two components. In the first place, the technocratic elite arose as young francophones, "unable to use their competence to advance in the anglophone-controlled private sector," concentrated instead "on circles of power which they were able to control."[19] In the second place, Quebecois capital provided the shoulders upon which the economic strategy of *rattrapage* (or catching up) was partially achieved. At the other end of the spectrum, Quebec also had a strong trade union movement, which survived despite rough treatment under Duplessis. The relationship between the Quebec state and the trade union movement has been ambivalent at best. While rapport was strong throughout the early 1960s, the discipline of power (and several recessions) meant that the unions clashed with both Liberal and Parti Québécois governments on numerous occasions. Nonetheless, compared to other provinces, Quebec's progressive labour legislation shows the clear influence of trade unions on government policy-making.

The manifestly economic and political programme of twentieth-century nationalism had one clear disadvantage, however: achievements made within Confederation dampened enthusiasm for autonomy. By the end of twentieth century, Quebecois could see that the strategy of *rattrapage* had been a success. As Marcel Rioux wrote as early as 1978, "The modernists agree that the Québécois have already liberated themselves from the institutions, ideas and values which kept them from progressing like their American and Canadian cousins."[20] If the neo-nationalist movement was based on the premise that Quebec could not succeed within federalism, they were proved wrong as long as "success" was defined purely in economic and political terms. But what more was there? Except for some vestigial traces, the Catholic Church no longer served as a frame of reference for French-Canadian identity. The French language continued to be a rallying point for nationalist sentiment in the second half of the twentieth century. However, as immigration levels to Quebec continue to increase, largely in the urban areas, the proportion of anglophones and allophones has become quite significant. The most emphatic challenge to Quebec nationalism at the beginning of the twenty-first century is, perhaps, the preservation of an ineffable Quebecois identity in an economically advanced and ethnically pluralist environment.

The pursuit of nationalism in a society that accepts a conception of citizenship based upon the principles of pluralism and the recognition of diverse identities, says Jacques Beauchemin, raises two substantial problems:

> The first problem is that the assertion of a citizenship open to particularist claims and recognizing the fragmentation of the political community questions the legitimacy of a nationalist project that is based on a specific shared history. The second problem is that this openness to pluralism does not eliminate to any extent the need to base the legitimacy of political action on the image of a political subject capable of symbolically transcending competition between particularisms when members of these identity groups lay their claims as a condition of fully achieving citizenship.[21]

Ironically, then, the overarching political challenge facing Quebec is very much the same one facing Canada as a nation: how is it possible to recognize many different identities but, at the same time, specify the qualities that define citizenship in the larger polity? The easiest answer is simply that citizenship is defined through geography; however, especially in a young country, geographical boundaries are arbitrary and have frequently been imposed through colonialism or conquest. Thus, the tension between identity and citizenship will likely be one of the most difficult political issues of the twenty-first century, both for Quebec, and for Canada.

NOTES

[1] Bélanger's online readings are an excellent and accessible source of Quebec history for English speakers. See "Readings in Quebec History," *Quebec History*, ed. Claude Bélanger, 20 August 2004, Marianopolis College, Montreal, PQ, 21 September 2005 <www2.marianopolis.edu/quebechistory/readings/index.htm>.

[2] See Kenneth McRoberts and Dale Posgate, *Quebec: Social Change and Political Crisis* (Toronto: McClelland and Stewart, 1980) 24–25.

[3] Claude Bélanger, "Readings in Quebec History: The Roman Catholic Church and Quebec," Quebec *History*, 23 August 2000, Marianopolis College, Montreal, PQ, 21 September 2005 <www2.marianopolis.edu/quebechistory/readings/church.htm>.

4 Joseph-Octave Plessis, "Sermon on Nelson's victory in Aboukir," *Canadian Political Thought,* ed. H.D. Forbes (Toronto: Oxford University Press, 1985) 6.

5 Louis-Joseph Papineau, quoted in Forbes, *Canadian Political Thought* 20.

6 Nelson Wiseman, "A note on 'Hartz-Horowitz at twenty': the case of French Canada," *Canadian Journal of Political Science* 21.4 (December 1988): 799.

7 H.D. Forbes, "Rejoinder to 'A note on "Hartz-Horowitz at twenty": the case of French Canada.'" *Canadian Journal of Political Science* 21.4 (December 1988): 807–08.

8 For a detailed but very readable account of the events leading up to Confederation, see Christopher Moore, *1867: How the Fathers Made a Deal* (Toronto: McClelland and Stewart, 1997).

9 Quoted in Jacques Monet, "LaFontaine," *Dictionary of Canadian Biography Online,* 2000,University of Toronto and Université Laval, 8 September 2005 <http://www.biographi.ca/EN/ShowBio.asp?BioId=38663>.

10 Monet, "LaFontaine," *Dictionary of Canadian Biography Online.*

11 Claude Bélanger, "Events, Issues, and Concepts of Quebec History—Quebec Nationalism: The Ultramontane Nationalism, 1840-1960," *Quebec History,* 23 August 2000, Marianopolis College, Montreal, PQ, 21 September 2005 <http://www2. marianopolis.edu/quebechistory/events/natpart3.htm>.

12 Bélanger, "Readings in Quebec History: The Roman Catholic Church and Quebec".

13 Bélanger, "Readings in Quebec History: The Roman Catholic Church and Quebec".

14 McRoberts and Posgate, *Quebec* 30.

15 Michel Brunet, "Trois dominantes de la pensée canadienne-française," *Études sur l'histoire et la pensée des deux Canadas* (Montreal: Beauchemin, 1958).

16 Brunet, "Trois dominantes" 27.

17 Denis Monière, "Currents of nationalism in Quebec," *Political Thought in Canada,* ed. Stephen Brooks (Toronto: Irwin Publishing, 1984) 165.

18 Alain-G. Gagnon, "The role of intellectuals in modern Quebec," *Political Thought in Canada,* ed. Stephen Brooks (Toronto: Irwin Publishing, 1984) 194.

19 Monière, "Currents of nationalism in Quebec" 180.

20 Marcel Rioux, *Quebec in Question,* trans. James Boake (Toronto: James Lorimer, 1978) 198.

21 Jacques Beauchemin, "What does it mean to be a Quebecer? Between self-preservation and openness to the other," *Québec: State and Society,* ed. Alain-G. Gagnon, 3rd ed. (Peterborough: Broadview Press, 2004) 23.

8 MINORITY RIGHTS AND MULTICULTURALISM

TWO NARRATIVES

"One might say," wrote Charles Taylor, "that the forces within Quebec that were always striving for a liberal society have won out." The year was 1991. "Perhaps," he added, "it would be more insightful to say that both parts of Canada have been swept up into the liberal consensus that has become established in the whole Western world in the wake of World War II." Why is it, he then asked, that "at the very moment when we agree upon so much, we are close to breakup in history, even though our values have never been so uniform"?[1] The values to which Taylor refers are those that, by and large, collectively constitute a distinct Canadian identity: greater respect for law and order, willingness to work collectively, and acceptance of regional equalization, multiculturalism, and entrenched rights. Paradoxically, agreement over these values only accentuates disagreement over one final point: the issue of what a nation is *for*. From the perspective of Quebec, argues Taylor, the "absolutely crucial" feature that Canada must have "is that it contribute to the survival and furtherance of *la nation canadienne-française.*"

This long-standing belief in cultural survival is what has led to the development of an alternative way of conceiving political governance in Canada. Much of the country, however, is still based very firmly upon the predominant "liberal" view of democracy, and this view, combined with the Canadian concern for cultural preservation, has led to a clash of rights theories that dominates the political agenda in Canada, and, increasingly, in other liberal democracies. How can we understand each perspective? Why does there seem to be such intransigence in ceding to the other's point of view? What are the points of disagreement? And is any reconciliation of views necessarily impossible?

One word of caution. The debate that has crept into Canadian political discourse, and which dominates Canadian political philosophy, is clearly a *philosophical* debate. It is not simply about morally enlightened citizens attempting to deal with the surly intransigence of uneducated boors. Most regions have an adequate supply of both kinds of individuals. One should not allow the rude and intolerant remarks that have been made in the course of this debate to obscure the fact that the debate consists of more than *one* interesting and profound account of how contemporary politics ought to be structured.

MINORITY RIGHTS: THE RECOGNITION OF "DEEP DIVERSITY"

Let us begin our discussion of these two narratives with Durham's *Report on the Affairs of British North America.* This is an arbitrary point of departure: there were certainly articulations of both liberal governance and collective cultural survival before 1839 in Canada. Durham's *Report,* however, is notable politically for two very important reasons: first, it stipulated the propriety of granting the liberal principles of governance to the colonies. This was no small matter. Responsible government was a step beyond colonial status to the development of formal nationhood, and it meant the clear (but not complete) attenuation of political control over Canada by Great Britain. But the second aspect of this report was much more controversial. Durham was quite clear that the proper future for Lower Canada was assimilation. His model was Louisiana, where the French-speaking inhabitants (many of whom were descended from the Acadians expelled from Nova Scotia by the British in 1755) were subject to "American" institutions and were expected to become active participants in the larger American community.

French Canadians were outraged and horrified. To them, Durham's *Report* was, like the 1763 proclamation, simply a restatement of the British conquest of 1760. Assimilation was not simply a form of political governance; it was the death of a living organism. Consequently, it was in the wake of the Durham Report that the link between liberal institutions and the threat of assimilation was made in the minds of many French Canadians. The fate of Riel and the fight for language rights in Manitoba, amongst other developments on the Canadian frontier, made it clear that the establishment of a secure French-Canadian community could only be considered within a clear geographical territory where French

Canadians remained a majority. For almost a century, the survival of the French-Canadian nation was considered in conjunction with that of the Roman Catholic Church. By the time of the Quiet Revolution, however, the "specificity" of the French-Canadian people had become both more complex and more political.

The attempt to understand and articulate a particular "Quebec identity" became a dominant project after the Catholic Church lost its hegemonic position over French-Canadian society. In the sixties, many discussions about a new Quebec identity were based upon the principles of socialism. The journal *Parti pris*, for example, articulated a vision of "a free, secular and socialist Quebec state," which defined an identity for French Canada separate from both Church and the assimilationist liberal institutions of English Canada.[2] Yet some intellectuals in Quebec realized, even during this time, that socialism alone was as insufficient a basis for a mature Quebec as was the Church or the deracinated liberal principles of Pierre Trudeau. In 1958, for example, sociologist Fernand Dumont published an essay that clearly recognized the importance of *culture* and the way in which individuals thought of themselves (and each other) within a particular context. "Le Canada français s'est défini au cours d'un passé qui pèse lourdement sur nous," he stated, and these historical events were reified to become part of an ongoing cultural identity: "on peut en effet supposer que si la part des groupes est trop inégale dans la définition de la communauté, ces groupes vont se reconnaître très inégalement dans la culture."[3]

Jocelyne Maclure has referred to Dumont as an example of "melancholic nationalism," a body of nationalist thinking that saw the Conquest as "a determinative stage in the establishment of a troubled, ambiguous, and negative self-concept."[4] The focus upon *identity*, at this point, was to a large extent influenced by two social trends evident in the early 1960s. The first was popularity of psychoanalysis and its application to broader social phenomena (in, for example, the works of Erich Fromm and Herbert Marcuse). The second was the decolonization of Africa. These two trends merged in the development of a psychology of political oppression. One proponent, Franz Fanon, argued in his 1961 book *Les Damnées de la Terre* that Algerians had internalized the identity of their colonial masters, an identity that was destroying them more painfully than any direct form of political oppression had. One can see similar ideas in Dumont's work:

In their determining moments French Canadians, according to Dumont, constantly fall back upon the solid ground that is constituted by the glance of the other in order not only to fight against ethnocide, but also to draw from it "the most solid representation of their identity." The appropriation of the image reflected by the other is, consequently, understood as being responsible for the contempt and hatred of the self that, according to Dumont, has animated francophones from Québec since their origin. The price of *survivance* resides in the atavistic and congenital sentiment of inferiority that is lived and felt by every new generation of Quebecer.[5]

However, the theorization of identity, and the way in which it justifies a special status for Quebec, was best articulated by Charles Taylor scant years later.

Taylor's understanding of Quebec's fears and aspirations was influenced not only by his own bicultural experience but also by his interest in Herder, Hegel, and the German Romantic tradition. This intellectual movement, a response to Enlightenment principles of rationalism, individualism, and universalism, looked more closely at how individuals were shaped by *social* constructs such as language, a common history, legal institutions, and so on. Hegel's analysis of how individuals, no less than societies, progress and develop through social interaction at various levels is clearly visible, for example, within Taylor's 1979 essay "Atomism"; and a Hegelian-inspired account of different varieties of "freedom" informs the influential, and provocative, essay "What's wrong with negative liberty" (also published in 1979).

Of these social constructs that shape individuals, the most significant is language. It is language, as the Romantics recognized, which "realizes man's humanity. Man completes himself in expression." Language is a highly social institution, not a solitary one: "Language is shaped by speech, and so can only grow up in a speech community. The language I speak, the web which I can never fully dominate and oversee, can never be just *my* language, it is always *our* language."[6] A philosophical system based upon individualism that ignores (or even negates) the crucial role of social relationships is thus poorly positioned to understand the nature of language. As a consequence, it is even more ill-suited to understand the moral and cultural aspects of human life upon which political institutions are, or ought to be, structured. People require a "plurality of goods" upon which to build and maintain a rich and satisfying life; yet liberal political philosophy is based upon assumptions of moral reduc-tionism, which do not even allow such goods to be considered in discussions of an ethically just system of political governance.[7]

One can see, then, why Taylor views the crisis of Quebec as a "failure of recognition." Liberal rights and freedoms do allow Quebecers to speak French if they so choose, but those steeped in the culture of atomism do not understand that *this is not a relevant point* for Quebecers. The point is, rather, "a matter of making sure that there is a community of people here in the future that will want to avail themselves of this opportunity."[8] The goal is a collec-tive one, and it cannot be achieved through the negative liberty provided by the rights of individuals.

But, a perplexed procedural liberal might ask, what *is* it, exactly, that is gained in the pursuit of a collective goal? The answer is twofold: security and dignity. The history of French Canada is replete with examples of both explicit and implicit strategies to assimilate French Canadians into a society in which they are no different from other citizens. The purpose of some degree of polit-ical autonomy, then, has always been to institutionalize the vigi-lance required to protect *la québécité*. The Quiet Revolution was premised on the idea that a strong Quebec state was the only way in which the French-speaking Quebecers within it could thrive, and, in the half-century since the Quiet Revolution, Quebecers have, on most socio-economic indicators, thrived indeed. Why, then, is the institutionalization of special status still such a burning issue?

In a democratic society, writes Taylor, the underlying premise is that *everyone* is accorded equal recognition. The humanity of modern liberal democracies is based upon the idea that the dignity of each person is respected; *that* is the justification for equal rights. Yet is being recognized as equally human all there is to dignity? Why can a sense of self-respect be so lacking amongst some people when formal political rights are granted to all? This phenomenon, argues Taylor, arises because we have failed to understand that dignity and self-respect do not simply depend upon being recognized for the ways in which we are all the same: no one, for example, finds much pride in the fact that they have one nose and ten fingers (although they might be uncomfortably self-conscious if they did not). Recognition, in a more profound sense, depends upon whether one's *distinct* qualities are acknowledged or dismissed, and particularly so if one sees these qualities as an essential part of oneself. Thus, "denied recognition can be a form of oppression":

> On a social plane, the understanding that identities are formed in open dialogue, unshaped by a predefined social script, has made the politics of equal recognition more central and stressful ... Equal recognition is not just the appropriate mode for a healthy democratic society. Its refusal can inflict damage on those who are denied it, according to a widespread modern view. The projecting of an inferior or demeaning image on another can actually distort and oppress, to the extent that it is interiorized.[9]

However, if this idea of "authenticity" is a crucial foundation for respect in modern society, it also leads to conceptual problems in a democratic one. The German Romantics may have had a resonant conception of the richness and complexities of human lives, but they were not restricted by the need to work within democratic institutions. Nonetheless, as Taylor states, "Equality is a notoriously difficult concept to apply and depends on the respect one makes salient." Developing a society in which important differences are both respected and protected, then, requires recognizing a "second-level" or "deep" diversity, "in which a plurality of ways of belonging would also be acknowledged and accepted."[10]

The task, then, is how to reconcile the formal equality upon which democracy, in principle, is based with the recognition of difference and diversity required by a modern pluralistic polity. It should be noted at this point that the history of political thought contains more than a few examples of liberal theories that were not democratic, and democratic theories that were not liberal. The eighteenth century, in particular, was populated by proponents of more liberal political and economic freedoms for citizens. Yet these more liberal measures had to be "contained" by fairly strong political institutions; the fear of social and political anarchy was strong enough that even the more liberal reformers did not favour making government dependent upon the fickle will of the mass of people. On the other hand, of course, radical democrats (like Rousseau) saw the will of the people as the *only* justifiable form of political authority; the real threat was in giving citizens unrestricted negative liberties to do whatever they wished, regardless of whether it was beneficial for themselves or for their community.

Modern liberal democracies have, at least since the twentieth century, generally accepted not only that "the will of the people" is not to be feared, but also that the will of the people *depends* upon the provision of substantial negative rights (rather than being corrupted by them). Still, some notable exceptions to this exist. The most intriguing is perhaps the "alternative conceptions" of democracy articulated by C.B. Macpherson in his 1965 Massey Lecture (later published as *The Real World of Democracy*). With considerable foresight, Macpherson challenged the belief that democratic institutions, together with a fundamental set of negative liberties, would result in a polity that was truly "democratic" in spirit as well as in a procedural sense. In the first place, he argues,

> when a substantial part of the society senses uneasily that it is dehumanized but does not know quite how, or when it is so dehumanized that only a few of the people at most can be expected to see that they are dehumanized, there is no use relying on the free votes of everybody to bring about a fully human society.[11]

In the second place, Macpherson stated, some societies simply "saw no intrinsic value in wealth-getting and gave no respect to the motive of individual gain. Equality and community, equality within a community, were traditionally rated more highly than individual freedom."[12] This, he says, is very much "the classic, pre-liberal" conception of democracy: "It is to make the criterion of democracy the achievement of ends which the mass of the people share and which they put ahead of separate individual ends."[13] These communities are democratic, but they are not liberal-democratic: "The one thing they have in common with liberal-democracy is the ultimate ideal of a life of freedom and dignity and moral worth for every member of the society."[14]

Macpherson's ideas did not, at the time, have a wide impact. Perhaps this was because of his unfortunate decision to articulate them at the height of the Cold War, when liberal democratic rights stood in clear opposition to the menace of authoritarianism (and specifically that of Communist regimes). They do merit attention now, however, not because of the success of socialism, which he espoused, but because of his portrayal of the weaknesses of liberal democracy. Macpherson's strategy of broadening our understanding of "democracy" to move beyond those based upon liberal principles was well ahead of his time. Interestingly, however, the current challenge to the same narrow model of liberal democracy to which Macpherson objected comes from broadening our understanding of the meaning of "liberalism," not of "democracy."

The aim of "liberal culturalists," who endeavour to include minority rights within liberal theory, is "to show that some (but not all) minority-rights claims enhance liberal values."[15] Such rights make liberalism more resonant, argues Will Kymlicka, because cultural communities provide a "context of choice" within which individuals can formulate constructive choices about the ways in which they wish to live their lives. Understanding cultural narratives, he states, "is a precondition of making intelligent judgements about how to lead our lives ... The availability of meaningful options depends upon access to a societal culture, and on understanding the history and language of that culture—its 'shared vocabulary of tradition and convention.'"[16] This position can be seen as part of the liberal tradition, which argues that certain conditions have to be present for individuals to act in a fully autonomous manner. Negative political rights are certainly the most obvious requirement; others have stipulated the importance of a liberal education, a certain minimum standard of material well-being, and even the presence of good health (or at least good health care). Given the considerable impact of the constitution of our identities upon the way in which we live our lives, why should they not be seen as a fundamental social "good" to which we can claim some entitlement?

Some theorists have concluded from this recognition of the significance of cultural communities to individuals that all cultures and identities must be accorded an equal measure of respect, or that those belonging to cultures or groups whose identities are devalued ought to be given special sets of rights (such as policy vetoes) that could counteract their political marginalization.[17] Others, however, are more conservative in their interpretation of the need for a constructive cultural context. Kymlicka, for example, believes that the argument for a "cultural" social good is only applicable to national minorities (i.e., those who have been involuntarily incorporated into a larger society.) Once we dismiss the idea that the liberal state is a neutral and objective institution that works equally for the benefit of all, it follows that national minorities have the same right to use the state actively to construct a society to their own advantage. Moreover, he argues, such societies are nonetheless limited, by the principles of liberalism, to the exercise of specific rights against a larger cultural group. They are enjoined from imposing illiberal "internal restrictions" upon members of their own group.[18]

There are several reasons that the narrative of minority rights has had considerably more success in Canada than in other nations (such as the United States). Canada's largest culturally distinct community lives in a geographic region in which they have generally been the majority. The more laissez-faire form of individualism favoured by most Americans has not permeated Canadian society as deeply. Also, Canada's system of federalism has accepted a relatively high level of regional self-governance, which, in turn, has been balanced by a fairly strong sense of collective responsibility. The latter has perhaps been as much the result of political opportunism as unmitigated general will, but the principle of sharing the burden to build a society of equals has endured regardless.

MULTICULTURALISM: THE PRIMACY OF FORMAL EQUALITY

More optimistically than provocatively, Kymlicka has noted that "this debate over justice is drawing to a close ... [I]n terms of the more general question of whether minority rights are inherently unjust, the debate is over, and the defenders of minority rights have won the day."[19] This optimistic view is, if anything, perhaps an accurate reflection of the fact that Canadian politics are still very much based upon the principle of elite accommodation, and political change, for better or for worse, is frequently instigated and shepherded by a critical mass of same-thinking elites.[20] One rather striking example of the possibility that public and elite opinion regarding minority rights may differ is the point made by Avigail Eisenberg: while national referenda show that majorities frequently "tend to support minority rights when minorities seek formal equality" (such as same-sex rights), referenda on distinct and discrete minority rights "are more likely to deepen cleavages rather than mend them."[21]

It may be, as Eisenberg argues, that national majorities tend to vote against discrete minority rights because referendum questions are framed in "the language of political equality" and thus provide a misleading and biased understanding of "what is at stake for minorities." On the other hand, as Catherine Frost asks, "[w]hat if these referendums are tapping into a genuine preference for undifferentiated equality or community rather than engendering it through manipulative framing or even through the demonstration effect of the referendum itself?"[22] One way of ensuring that referendum participants ratify the "right" answer, she suggests, is to structure the debate "in a way that avoids reinforcing a limited view of what justice looks like."[23] This strategy may be a sound method of ensuring that both accounts of "justice" are fairly articulated. And even if such a practice tended to "privilege" a view of distinct minority rights over that of formal equality, one could always observe that this was, in the manner of Rousseauean democracy, simply a way of helping people to understand the general will. We do not always accept majority views unquestioningly: even the most old-fashioned liberal would not accept the decision of a majority if it conflicted with "accepted" principles of justice (if, for example, the majority voted to remove the constitutional rights of any particular minority). Where the case of discrete minority rights is different, however, is that it addresses the *interpretation* of democracy itself, rather than merely its application. If a majority consistently refuses to accept a redefinition of democracy, then, does this mean that the majority are insufficiently enlightened, or does it mean that a different way of understanding democracy would be unacceptable to them *however* much they were educated about it?

An account of liberal democracy based upon formal equality may thus prove, at a wider level, to be more resistant to change than liberal culturalists believe. The more traditional narrative based upon universalism, political equality, and some conceptual distinction between a "public" and "private" sphere has been slow to respond to the challenges posed to it. However, the history of Canada has itself been a continuous dialectic between the protection of cultural homogeneity and liberal pluralism. Durham's strategy of assimilation, as Janet Ajzenstat has argued, may have been divisive, and it may well have caused a great deal of rancour between French and English Canadians. But it was not a naive or ill-conceived plan—the response of French Canadians made it clear that *they* felt it was eminently possible to be assimilated–nor was the plan divorced from an account based firmly upon a clear sense of justice. To allow the French Canadians to remain a separate minority, believed Durham, would simply make them increasingly vulnerable to exploitation by an economically and politically powerful majority. The only way to ensure that French Canadians had the same political opportunities as the English Canadians, by this account, was to encourage them away from a rural, agrarian life into one in which all political and economic opportunities remained open for them. This assimilative impulse, as Ajzenstat points out, followed directly from a tenet of seventeenth-century liberal thought in which "the conquered were as entitled to participate as the conquerors." Consequently, if there were to be political institutions in the colonies based upon responsible government, then French Canadians were to be given positions in them "on the same basis as the English."[24]

It is unsurprising that the policy-makers of the day decided to split the difference and, while agreeing to a geographically distinct unit of political governance for the French Canadians, insist that it be governed according to British principles of responsible government. In fact, it may be that this British liberal institution itself was largely the reason that French Canadian culture was able to survive as well as it did. Also interesting is that the best articulation of liberal principles in Canada, as well as of modern Quebecois nationalism, arose in response to the way in which the province was governed in the middle of the twentieth century. French Canadians under Duplessis were palpably worse off in terms of economic and political opportunities than most other Canadians. However, the issue for Quebecers, as it was for Durham, was whether the solution rested in greater or less participation in Canadian liberal democracy. Therefore, while the Quebecois nationalists of the sixties argued that Quebec could only flourish if the province had more control over its economic, social, and political concerns, Quebecois liberals stated, like Durham, that individuals in the province would be better off it they were given more equal status as *Canadians*.

The strongest voice for liberal rather than nationalist reform was *Cité Libre*, a publication founded by intellectuals and civil rights workers in 1950. While the contributors were provoked initially by the heavy-handed political tactics of the Union Nationale, the *citélibrists* became increasingly concerned by the current of nationalism that began to influence thinking in the province. One of the most notable contributors to *Cité Libre* was Pierre Elliott Trudeau, who argued in no ambivalent terms that cultural nationalism would simply mean more intense marginalization as a society and fewer opportunities for individuals within such a society. If French Canadians were concerned for their language, or believed that they were disadvantaged because they did not speak English, then the solution was to reinvigorate the constitutional guarantees already offered by the constitution and to "place the English and French languages on a basis of absolute judicial equality." But Trudeau's most biting criticism of Quebec nationalism was grounded in his observation—quite justifiable in 1958—that nationalism was being used as a reason to ignore the tenets of democracy. French-Canadian culture was surviving, but at a terrible and shameful cost to the individuals within it.

Trudeau was very well acquainted with the ultramontane nationalism that still dominated Quebec in the first half of the twentieth century; he understood that Lionel Groulx's dictum that "French Canadians must understand their own past" could also be used against the conservative nationalist hegemony. The absolutism of the Bourbon kings, suggested Trudeau, was hardly a better alternative for Quebec than the liberalism of the English. Autonomy was dangerous if it were untempered by democracy. "French Canadians," he noted,

are perhaps the only people in the world who "enjoy" democracy without having had to fight for it ... As Durham later remarked, they were being initiated to responsible government at the wrong end; a people who had not been entrusted with the governing of a parish were suddenly enabled through their votes to influence the destinies of the state.[25]

Trudeau's most obvious political opponent on Quebec was René Lévesque. Lévesque rejected the view that Quebec nationalism meant ultramontane nationalism. "For a very long time," admitted Lévesque, "we have allowed our public administration to stagnate in negligence and corruption, and left our political life in the hands of fast talkers and our own equivalent of those African kings who grew rich by selling their own tribesmen." The goal, he stated, was to build a society "as progressive, as efficient, and as 'civilized' as any in the world."[26] With the benefit of hindsight, however, one can see that Lévesque's argument for sovereignty was based upon two quite distinct kinds of arguments. On the one hand, he makes the Herderian argument that a culture is fundamentally constitutive of distinct qualities that must be maintained irrespective of political or economic well-being:

> *We* know and feel that these are the things that make us what we are. They enable us to recognize each other wherever we may be. This is our own special wave-length on which, despite all interference, we can tune each other in loud and clear, with no one else listening.[27]

However, Lévesque also argues at length that it is federal control over economic and social policy-making that continues to keep the people of Quebec marginalized both in terms of material well-being and political influence. Lévesque's point is that Quebec citizens ought to be no worse off than the English-speaking minority in Quebec: that they ought, in other words, to have a formal equality of opportunity with English Quebecers.

It is difficult to judge with assurance which strategy—nationalist or liberal—has been responsible for Quebec's renaissance. Certainly, Quebec's policy of state-led development contributed to the modernization of the province and to its increased political influence, although Trudeau's insistence at facilitating Quebec at the federal level undoubtedly was a variable as well. The debate over Quebec is thus quite different now than it was when Trudeau and Lévesque presented quite distinct visions about the future of the province. Modern Quebec is able to negotiate from a much stronger political position, even as its justification for secession becomes much more complex. No longer can Quebec easily prove that its socio-economic position within Confederation is markedly inferior; nor can it reference a clear, homogeneous culture that must be protected from the intrusions of modernity or liberalism.

Thus, Trudeau's greatest intellectual opponent is likely not Lévesque but Charles Taylor. Comfortable with problems of political and moral complexity, Taylor continues to argue that simple equality is as unacceptable to Quebec now as it was fifty years ago:

> To build a country for everyone, Canada would have to allow for second-level or "deep" diversity, in which a plurality of ways of belonging would also be acknowledged and accepted. Someone of, say, Italian extraction in Toronto or Ukrainian extraction in Edmonton might indeed feel Canadian as a bearer of individual rights in a multicultural mosaic. His or her belonging would not "pass through" some other community, although the ethnic identity might be important to him or her in various ways. But this person might nevertheless accept that a Québécois or a Cree or Déné might belong in a very different way, that these persons were Canadian through being members of their national communities. Reciprocally, the Québécois, Cree, or Déné would accept the perfect legitimacy of the "mosaic" identity.[28]

Opponents of the idea of "deep diversity" or minority rights remain sceptical of this position.

The minority-rights argument, again, is that policies that treat groups differently in response to their unique cultural affiliation are, at a meta-level, actually treating them "equally" in what matters most to them. Admittedly, the philosophical substance of this argument is both dense and complex, as is the philosophical response to it, and one choosing to pursue the debate more closely would be well advised to consult the multitude of books on the subject.[29] One can, however, identify at least three major objections to the argument for the political institutionalization of "deep diversity." The first is that the premise of this argument—that liberal democracy is inherently universalizing and homogenizing—is simply false. Partly a legacy of postmodern theorization, this premise holds that, because liberalism is based upon the principles of universalism and equality, the establishment of liberal institutions requires that all individuals subject to liberal laws and institutions become completely alike in all ways. Individuals become identical and interchangeable ciphers, as what is distinctive about each person has been swept away in the move toward universal conformity.

This assumption, argue its critics, shows a marked lack of historical understanding, as one of the reasons that liberalism was developed as a workable political doctrine in the first place was in order to accommodate numerous and incommensurable differences in religious observance. There are those, they recognize, who argue that the spread of liberal democracy was simply a guise for imperialist and assimilationist policies, and there is good evidence to show that not all who espoused liberal democratic principles were the kindest or most honest people. However, continues the critique, the historical record does not in itself show that liberal tenets necessarily reduce to assimilation and dull conformity. (At worst, this record shows that cognitive dissonance is not a recent phenomenon; consider the "good liberals" who did their best to deny "universal" rights to women or to certain races.) It may be true that liberalism stipulates that all individuals be treated "equally" and that this principle, in practice, means that all individuals are given the same set of rights to the same kinds of things. This principle does not, they hasten to add, preclude the idea of affirmative action, which recognizes that some people are so disadvantaged that they cannot profit from the equal distribution of rights. It does stipulate, however, that, when the condition of any disadvantaged group improves, the need for affirmative action is gone and any special provisions are removed. Thus, far from leading to a condition of stultifying sameness, liberal rights are designed to permit as great a space as possible in which to assert one's uniqueness without sanction or penalty.

The second objection held by critics of deep diversity is thus that a system of liberal rights is in fact sufficient to allow for a minimally decent life. But is this "decency" too minimal? What of the argument that the negative freedoms (to speech, to association, to religious observance, to vote, and so on) and positive rights (provided by the Canadian system of health care, education, and social welfare) are simply not meaningful to those who require a *specific* social structure—an identifiable culture—in order to live their lives well? The first response to this argument is that there is nothing in liberal democratic doctrine that necessarily *precludes* such a cultural context, unless such cultural practices involve behaviour that cannot be condoned by liberal societies. (Some of these practices—such as wearing a veil—can arguably be justified by saying that those involved consent to these practices; other more extreme practices— such as ritual human sacrifice—could never be permitted regardless of any articulation of consent. Hard cases, obviously, would fall between these two extremes).

The second response to the argument that liberal freedoms and rights are not necessarily meaningful to minorities is that having to lead an "unmeaningful" liberal life would be similar to a talented piano player who could not afford the lessons that could make her a professional musician: certainly unfortunate, but not obviously unjust. The system of liberal rights were designed in the first place with the assumption that political conflict (and a great deal of blood-shed) could only be avoided if issues of spiritual and psychological fulfilment were kept out of the domain of political governance. Since the veracity of religious requirements could not be substantiated rationally, but were matters of faith, all lifestyles contributing to eternal salvation should properly be left to individuals and their churches.

What of those, however, who, through no fault of their own, find significant aspects of their culture foreclosed upon them? If they have been used to a particular context of meaningfulness only to have it removed, is this not unjust? This argument leads critics of deep diversity to a third objection. It is relatively (though not always) clear when one is denied the freedom to speak or to organize a group or to cast a vote. It is also relatively (though not always) clear when one is being deprived of the minimum material needs one requires to stay alive. These requirements are subject to a relatively objective account of what is required in each case. But "leading a meaningful life"? The argument that cultural contexts ought to be protected because they impart a sense of meaningfulness is much more difficult to judge impartially. If culture is defined as a way of seeing one's life, then it is, as Barry argues, merely tautology to argue that cultures ought to be given special status *because* they allow one to understand one's life a certain way.[30]

It may be the strange confluence between nineteenth-century Romanticism and late twentieth-century postmodernism that has led political theorists to consider the role that "identity" plays in debates about justice. But it has been the application of the very liberal concept of "equal respect" to the notion of identity that has led to the claim that, as one's identity is integral to one's sense of self-respect, one can logically demand equal respect for the culture that imparts one's identity. The liberal demand for equal respect was, however, based upon the fact that individuals were once treated quite differently in the application of *fundamental* political rights, so theorists believed that securing "equal respect" could be achieved through the establishment of equal political rights. Whether you felt as good about yourself as your neighbour did depended upon how you wished to live your life. Since then, however, the basis of respect has become tremendously subjective. As workplace managers discovered throughout the 1980s and 1990s, it is difficult to determine before the fact what it means to each person to "feel respected."

There is thus still considerable unease at taking liberalism "a step farther" and going beyond the general stipulation that all individuals possess an equal set of rights. The justification for, and the objections to, such a modified liberalism now comprise the dominant lines of debate within Canadian political thought. It is unclear which of these two narratives is now the "orthodoxy": certainly the provision of self-government and minority rights in numerous cases seems to show that the narrative of minority rights is becoming increasingly accepted. However, the resistance to such policies seems to illustrate that others believe that a society based upon liberal multiculturalism is not only adequate but also more just.

It does the country great disservice to claim that either account is based solely upon intolerance or political opportunism. Most people will likely take the position they do because one of the narratives noted above makes more sense to them than the other. One must also recognize that the particular historical challenges of each region will influence how individuals weigh the threats or advantages of each respective narrative. Those in Quebec, for example, have no lack of examples to point to in arguing that assimilation is, to them, a palpable threat. Westerners remember the power and influence of the central Canadian oligopolies that controlled so much of the capital upon which the West relied, and they see the implementation of orthodox liberal democracy as one of the factors that effectively diminished the political and economic power of established central Canadian power blocs.

Some have argued that the model of liberal multiculturalism is the more "American" version of modern democracy (the "melting pot" model, as we were taught in grade school, as opposed to the Canadian "mixing pot").[31] Others dispute the facile assumption that Canada was historically an agglomeration of organic traditions in contrast to the Whig or the American liberal traditions. As Ajzenstat points out, for example, the influx of American Loyalists into Canada challenged Tory beliefs rather than bolstering them:

the Loyalists "didn't come to the British territories hoping to find a society where they could bow at the knee and doff the cap."[32] Still, it is likely that the narrative of minority rights has a distinct advantage simply insofar as it is distinct from American liberalism. That this explanation lacks philosophical rigour may be less important than the fact that it does clearly distinguish a form of "Canadian liberalism" or, in Michael Ignatieff's words, a "noble experiment" watched by the rest of the world as a test of whether a country divided by ethnicity can not only survive but prosper.[33] Critics may sniff that a successful system of minority rights may tell us nothing more than that philosophical inconsistencies will not destabilize a confident democracy. However, Canada has, in various ways, been a country that has had to reflect for a long time about how (or whether) to accommodate discrete groups of citizens, and, regardless of the outcome, the process of reflection itself must necessarily shape Canadian society and Canadian political thought.

NOTES

[1] Charles Taylor, "Shared and divergent values," *Reconciling the Solitudes: Essays on Canadian Federalism and Nationalism,* ed. Guy Laforest (Montreal and Kingston, McGill-Queen's University Press, 1993) 156.

[2] For a brief discussion of the role of the *Parti pris* see Alain-G. Gagnon, "The role of the intellectuals in modern Quebec: the drive for social hegemony," *Political Thought in Canada,* ed. Stephen Brooks (Toronto: Irwin Publishing, 1984) 200–03.

[3] Fernand Dumont, "De quelques obstacles à la prise de conscience chez les Canadiens français," *Le rouge et le bleu: une anthologie de la pensée politique au Québec de la Conquête à la Révolution tranquille,* ed. Yvan Lamonde and Claude Corbo (Montreal: Les Presses de l'Université de Montréal, 1999) 520. This essay was, interestingly, originally published in *Cité Libre* in 1958.

[4] Jocelyne Maclure, "Narratives and counter-narratives of identity in Quebec," *Québec: State and Society,* ed. Alain-G. Gagnon, 3rd ed. (Peterborough: Broadview Press, 2004) 37.

[5] Maclure, "Narratives" 37–38. Maclure quotes Dumont's *Genèse de la société québécoise* (Montreal: Boréal, 1996).

[6] Charles Taylor, "Language and human nature," *Philosophical Papers I: Human Agency and Language* (Cambridge: Cambridge University Press, 1985) 233–34.

[7] See Charles Taylor, "The diversity of goods," *Philosophical Papers II: Philosophy and the Human Sciences* (Cambridge: Cambridge University Press, 1985) 230–47.

[8] Taylor, "Shared and divergent values" 176.

[9] Charles Taylor, *The Malaise of Modernity* (Concord, ON: Anansi Press, 1991) 49–50.

[10] Taylor, "Shared and divergent values" 180, 183.

[11] C.B. Macpherson, *The Real World of Democracy* (Toronto: CBC Enterprises, 1983) 19–20.

[12] Macpherson, *The Real World* 23.

[13] Macpherson, *The Real World* 29.

[14] Macpherson, *The Real World* 30.

[15] Will Kymlicka, "The new debate over minority rights," *Canadian Political Philosophy:*

Contemporary Reflections, ed. Ronald Beiner and Wayne Norman (Don Mills, ON: Oxford University Press Canada, 2001) 163.

[16] Will Kymlicka, *Multicultural Citizenship* (Oxford: Clarendon Press, 1995) 83.

[17] See, for example, I.M. Young, "Polity and group difference: a critique of the ideal of universal citizenship," *Ethics* 99.2 (1989): 250-74.

[18] Kymlicka, "The new debate over minority rights" 163.

[19] Kymlicka, "The new debate over minority rights" 169.

[20] As Brian Barry has responded to the idea that minority rights advocates have won the day, "What is true is that those who actually write about the subject do so for the most part from some sort of multiculturalist position. But the point is that those who do not take this position tend not to write about it at all but work instead on other questions that they regard as more worthwhile. Indeed, I have found that there is something approaching a consensus among those who do not write about it that the literature of multiculturalism is not worth wasting powder and shot on." Brian Barry, *Culture and Equality: An Egalitarian Critique of Multiculturalism* (Cambridge, MA: Harvard University Press, 2001) 6.

[21] Avigail Eisenberg, "When (if ever) are referendums on minority rights fair?" *Representation and Democracy Theory*, ed. David Laycock (Vancouver and Toronto: UBC Press, 2004) 7, 5.

[22] Catherine Frost, "Getting to yes: people, practices, and the paradox of multicultural democracy," *Representation and Democratic Theory*, ed. David Laycock (Vancouver and Toronto: UBC Press, 2004) 54.

[23] Frost, "Getting to yes" 60.

[24] Janet Ajzenstat, "Liberalism and assimilation: Lord Durham reconsidered," *Political Thought in Canada*, ed. Stephen Brooks (Toronto: Irwin Publishing, 1984) 239-257. For a more detailed account, see Ajzenstat, *The Political Thought of Lord Durham* (Montreal and Kingston: McGill-Queen's University Press, 1988).

[25] Pierre Elliott Trudeau, "Some obstacles to democracy in Quebec," *Federalism and the French Canadians* (Toronto: Macmillan, 1968) 103-04.

[26] René Lévesque, *An Option for Quebec* (Toronto: McClelland and Stewart, 1968) 17.

[27] Lévesque, *An Option for Quebec* 15.

[28] Charles Taylor, "Shared and divergent values" 180, 183.

[29] A good place to begin would be to read Will Kymlicka's *Multicultural Citizenship: A Liberal Theory of Minority Rights* (Oxford: Clarendon Press, 1995) together with Brian Barry's *Culture and Equality: An Egalitarian Critique of Multiculturalism* (Cambridge, MA: Harvard University Press, 2001).

[30] Barry, *Culture and Equality* 253.

[31] See, for example, Will Kymlicka, "American multiculturalism in the international arena," *Dissent* (Fall 1998): 73-79.

[32] Janet Ajzenstat, *The Once and Future Canadian Democracy* (Montreal and Kingston: McGill-Queen's University Press, 2003) 6.

[33] See an excerpt of Ignatieff's speech to the 2005 Liberal Convention in *The Globe and Mail* 4 March 2005 : A13.

The map of ideas painted here has been presented as a discrete set of currents cascading together to form something called "Canadian political thought." But history rarely presents itself so neatly. Ideas do not simply follow each other in clear chronological succession, nor do they take great care not to interfere with each other. To be presented more accurately, these streams of thought should be smudged and blurred so that the ideas run together as if left out in a soft rain. Nor are the currents of thought noted here exhaustive. Recent interpretations of nineteenth-century Canadian history, for example, are focusing more intently upon the possibility of a civic republican tradition. This approach, like Tory collectivism, is based more upon the community than the individual. Also, like Toryism, it refuses to embrace rationalism as a foundational principle. But civic republicanism is egalitarian, not organic, and its pursuit of virtue is not necessarily based strictly upon tradition. The icon of civic republicanism is Rousseau, not Burke, and the value it places upon ideals of "democracy" is unsurprisingly greater.

Other streams of thought have been neglected here altogether. The legacy of anarchist thought, for example, is probably under-examined in Canada, as are the strands of traditional aboriginal ideas about political governance. Still, one might insist, with old-fashioned rationalist persistence, what is it that ties everything together? What is it that makes Canada *unique* as a polity? For we are. Our ideas and values shape our institutions, and these institutions in turn have a clear impact upon what we promote and tolerate. (If pollsters are correct, for example, we would certainly have elected John Kerry over George Bush.) How can we account for the way in which we are different from any other country, and especially from the United States whose influence upon us has been the most pervasive in the past century?

Those who rely upon the explanation of a "tory touch" would say that Canadians simply value security and stability more highly than freedom. As others suggest, though, a more accurate interpretation is that Canadians comprehend the value of a slightly different *kind* of freedom. The Romantic tradition in political theory has articulated an account of freedom quite distinct from the liberal idea that freedom is the absence of external constraints or forces upon an individual. In the well-established tradition of Rousseau, Hegel, Marx, and Nietzsche, for example, freedom is a condition or state of mind that requires a very specific set of circumstances to attain. The absence of physical impediments, in Rousseau's words, leads to mere licentiousness, not to liberty. What *is* needed to achieve liberty is slightly different in each account. Rousseau, for example, argues that citizens cannot be free unless they have the understanding and the willingness to make decisions according to the common good rather than personal interest. This account is not as foreign to modern sensibilities as one might believe; those who have teenagers, for example, know that the autonomy of these young adults is dependent not only upon achieving particular skills but upon the development of a certain degree of insight and maturity that allows them to use their knowledge in a certain way. Psychologists, too, know that adults labouring in a state of emotional turmoil cannot take advantage of their legal and political rights as fully as those not enduring such a state.

In Nietzsche's view, freedom rested upon one's ability to see one's world in a creative and unique way. Marx's account of freedom, of course, was based upon the observation that negative political liberties meant a great deal less to those trapped in poverty. Property rights, as those on the Left have argued ever since, are useless to those with no property to protect. Besides, if one accepts Marx's argument that an individual's creativity is the most constitutive aspect of one's identity, then even a well-paid job of boring monotony is an obstacle to a "free" existence. This account has become unfashionable in recent decades. We still sympathize with those whose poverty traps them in a life of drudgery, but, we argue, the idea of basing rights upon the presumption that creativity is integral to identity cannot be proven and is thus suspect. Interestingly, however, current generations of political theorists are comfortable in arguing, again with more rhetoric than evidence, that cultural practices are inherently constitutive of individual identity and must therefore be protected with discrete rights.

The popularity of this particular argument will likely continue for some time. What is worth noting here is that what acts as a consistent motif in a great deal of Canadian political thought is the belief that "freedom" must be understood as something beyond the liberal manifestation of negative individual liberty. This is not to say that such an account is the *dominant* idea underlying Canadian political thought: we are, as Ajzenstat points out, very similar to the United States (and to Great Britain) insofar as we are *predominantly* based upon an account of political governance that stresses the protection of individual liberties, the selection of leaders through regular elections, and a political process that is, as much as possible, transparent and accountable. We are, in other words, fundamentally a liberal democracy, and likely to remain so for the conceivable future.

However, as Freud noted, the small differences rather than the great similarities can be most important to us. This is especially so in matters of national identity. Canada is an unrepentant liberal democracy, but certain aspects of liberalism have been tweaked. Kymlicka has argued that it is not a refutation of liberalism but its reinterpretation that has defined the interest in minority rights. In the same way, this account does not reject the idea of "freedom" in and of itself, but holds, as do Taylor and others, that the conceptualization of freedom ought not to be limited to the idea that it is simply the absence of physical impediments. Freedom, in this account, is a condition that needs to be nurtured and developed very carefully by the society itself. The exercise of self-interest, rather than being a manifestation of freedom, is evidence of a clear lack of political maturity. Individuals must be able to think of the wider social good before they can make constructive political decisions, and they cannot learn to do so if they are enveloped in an ideological fog that not only glorifies individual choices but also refuses to tolerate any social constraints on them. Thus, the new emphasis upon minority rights not only is crucial in facilitating meaningful individual choices but also tempers the choices individuals make by bringing to them an awareness of the fragility and complexity of the social organism that sustains them.

The principles underlying theories of minority rights thus have a long historical pedigree. The current articulation of minority rights is novel, but the ideas underlying it are not. It is, in this way, far too simple merely to say that "the Tory tradition" is itself responsible for the interest in and support for minority rights. To the extent that contemporary minority rights theories are influenced by past traditions, these traditions are from the Romantic period, and were developed in response to liberal ideals. It may be that a Tory sensibility—such as a greater tolerance for authority—has meant a greater tolerance for minority rights, but the theory itself is clearly grounded in modern, not feudal, ideas.

The nature of Canadian identity, however, goes well beyond this tolerance. The claim that a Canadian identity ought to consist of a multiplicity of identities does not simply reduce to a formal recognition for minority rights, and alternatives to the minority-rights account are not exhausted by the single, all-encompassing liberal worldview (which many call the "American" approach). There is another, more subtle approach that is definitively Canadian, and one might almost think of this as an "anti-identity" identity. Rather than flaunting the concept of "identity" at all (either as a monolithic patriotic construct or as a small discrete affiliation), the emphasis in this account is much more upon simply *getting on*. Different ways of doing things are tolerated, but they are not advertised, promoted, or celebrated as much as they are practised. It is as bad form to flaunt one's "identity" unnecessarily as it is to parade one's income. The quiet acceptance of a natural diversity is as crucial to this account as the forceful politicking is a part of the multiple-identity account of Canadian identity.

It is this rejection of identity politics that is, if anything, the true descendant of "Toryism" in Canada. The concept of Toryism does accept the existence of separate cultural groups insofar as there is no necessary philosophical link between imperialism and Toryism. The latter assumes that a social and political community can only exist as a stable entity over time if there is a shared history of customs and traditions that ties citizens together and allows them to make sense of each other's actions and utterings. Equality, according to this account, is not necessary, nor is the reduction of any of these customs to a rational explanation of behaviour. Thus a Tory understands completely why other cultures exist, and there may well be a willingness to let these communities be (especially if it would unsettle one's own society to interfere with them). A defence of one's own society is, in the same way, a perfectly comprehensible explanation for militaristic behaviour. But there is no discussion of "equal respect for cultures" or "meaningful contexts of choice for individuals" in this account of Toryism.

In Canada, imperialism and Toryism are frequently conjoined; it was, after all, Britain's imperial policy that brought "Tory traditions" to Canada. But by the time Britain had truly become an imperial power, it was also very much exhibiting the traits of a liberal society. By the middle of the eighteenth century, Britain had solidly established its political presence in the Canadian colonies. At this time in Britain, the Industrial Revolution was in full throttle, and the social and political institutions were undergoing massive transformations. Britain's imperial design was part of this political conversion. Of course, people themselves do not simply become transformed into "liberals" overnight (or even over a decade). Attitudes and customs change much more slowly than political objectives, and it is hardly surprising that colonists settling in a vast and threatening environment should want to hold more tightly to their traditions than those left behind. It is, consequently, not impossible to talk about "the Tory tradition" in Canada, but this stream of Toryism had little interest in championing the rights of the marginalized. *This* was, and still is, the role of liberalism (and, of course, radicalism) in Canada.

Thus contemporary political thought in Canada has two forms. There is the vigorous debate over minority rights, which is derived from the Romantic reaction against liberal ideals. Then there is the phlegmatic Canadian pragmatism, which doubts that this modern insistence on defining some clear "identity" is really a good thing at all. This pragmatic view is the genuine Tory perspective. "Identity," according to Tories, is not something that you protect for the future; it is only what you can see in retrospect. True Tories would be appalled by the claim that identity must be defined or set in advance; it can, they would argue, only arise over a long period of time from the day-to-day travails of a society's inhabitants. And no one can predict that.

This debate between "tories" and "liberals" is in fact a critical component of the development of Canadian political thought; although, as I have sketched here, it has been improperly understood. This misunderstanding is hardly surprising, as the Tory suspicion of the reification of "culture" tends to end up (rather paradoxically) as a defence of liberal institutions. This defence is not in itself incoherent; in fact, it has good historical precedent. The arch-Tory Edmund Burke himself looked to the settlement of 1689, and not to arbitrary monarchical absolutism, as the set of principles on which conservatism was to be based. The epistemological conservatism of Burke (like that of Hume) was well suited to the constraints on central power secured by the proto-liberal constitutional settlement of 1689 because the latter secured to a certain extent the political space necessary for the stable (if unpredictable) social development of organic communities.

Again, one must stress that intellectual currents are not insular phenomena that are protected by time, taste, or good manners from bumping against each other. They collide, interact, borrow from each other, and then diverge again as their proponents work through what aspects are most important to them. Similarities arise even when they are not deliberately constructed. The minority-rights approach, despite its liberal genealogy, has clearly been influenced by the Left in its insistence that the dynamics of power in concrete situations limit the abstract advantages of the negative rights propounded by more classical liberals. It is the fact that minorities are (by definition) small that they are vulnerable to losing their "context of choice" as they become absorbed into the mainstream. (This, for example, was the theme of Robert Paul Wolff's radical 1965 essay on toleration, which simply argued that "tolerance" in itself was not necessarily a good thing if it allowed toxic relations of power already existing to continue unchecked.[1]) The same classical liberals, of course, would respond that they are unpersuaded that a discrete cultural context of choice is as essential to human life (just as they are unpersuaded that the need for creative work is crucial). While both are desirable, they argue, neither is essential; a universal schedule of liberal rights is quite appropriate for preserving the fundamental structure of governance for the free activity of citizens.

The intellectual history of Canada is messy, but it is interesting. But has it been a *good thing*? Evaluation of overarching political theories is tricky because (so the saying goes) where one stands depends very much on where one is sitting. Certainly our particular debate has made us more aware that political institutions should avoid assuming that social life is completely atomized. But to what extent do our present institutions do this? Despite what some communitarians (and even some minority rights proponents) have claimed, liberalism does not assume that we must aim for a life in which detached individuals only connect with each other through some formal contract. When liberalism was developed as a political theory, the presence of organic communities was such an established reality that no one assumed that the social bonds between people in a single society could ever be utterly broken or formalized. The social contract was simply a rhetorical device; although Hobbes's tongue-in-cheek suggestion that individuals simply spring from the ground like mushrooms in a damp forest has undoubtedly caused contemporary liberals no little grief.

Hobbes's quip about individuals aside, there is good reason to suppose that liberals took the human bonds between individuals as a given and simply tried to figure out how these social and psychological ties could be balanced by a set of blind laws that mitigated the favouritism and prejudice of close communities. It is doubtful that Hobbes, or Locke, or even John Stuart Mill could have imagined that societies could have become as solipsistic and deracinated as they have. And yet they *have* become highly atomistic. Is "liberalism" responsible? If so, what ought to be done to counter the anomie and despair? The current thinking argues that liberalism is to blame and that a hefty dose of culture is the proper tonic. However, the entire focus upon "equality rights versus minority rights" (or Liberalism versus Romanticism) is the assumption that cultural identity and liberal freedoms are the only substantial variables in this debate.

This assumption is simplistic. The great disconnects in modern life are not caused just by a lack of cultural ties, and the protection of discrete cultural traditions will likely have little effect on these problems. There has been a notable tradition in twentieth-century Canadian political thought that emphasizes the relationship between the market, technology, and social life; and this angle has been noticeably missing since all the intellectual tools covered with the dust of Marxism have been discarded. Canada has produced a fascinatingly iconoclastic stream of critical political thought including Harold Innis, Marshall McLuhan, C.B. Macpherson, David Gauthier, and G.A. Cohen. This current has never been subsumed within the stream of orthodox Marxism or traditional social democracy, as each theorist has taken various observations about materialism, capitalism, contractualism, technology, and so on but has attempted to think about them in a less rigidly constrained way. Formal Marxism may not have much more to say to contemporary audiences than that some people are rich and some are poor and that the former have a great deal more power than the latter. Current generations are rightfully wary of trading either liberal rights or cultural contexts for the dangerous edifices of orthodox Marxism. Also, these same fears have made us wary of thinking about the relationship between the market and modern society. Yet neither the espousal of liberal rights (essential though they are) nor the demand for minority rights (humane though *they* are) have anything to say either about how to harness the powerful potential of contemporary economic forces or about how to mitigate its worst excesses. Discussing cultural identity (or postmodernism or romanticism) is probably a lot more fun than figuring out ways in which international political institutions can be designed to regulate international capital flows while remaining accountable to local populations. These more enjoyable discussions, however, are perhaps taking far too much attention away from the pragmatic solutions that may be available for pressing economic or ecological problems.

Canadian political thought, in sum, is far more complex than simply going from "Tory" to "tolerance." Tolerance in Canada has developed (rather slowly) as part of the liberal democratic sensibility that enveloped most of the Western world, and the "tolerance for minority rights" (which is what many mean when looking at twenty-first century Canadian thought) grew out of the Romantic opposition to perceptions of liberal uniformity and rationalistic homogeneity. Toryism in Canada has been a curmudgeonly suspicion of all things that are too new, too destabilizing, or epistemologically arrogant. Canada's Tory touch has resulted in a society that has produced far fewer instances of "progress" or novelty; however, it has produced a society stable enough to withstand some quite radical public policies. This phlegmatic and temperate demeanour, combined with the humanism of the liberal tradition, has grown into a political maturity that allows the country to function in a fairly stable and open manner. This transcendent quality, in the end, may reflect more favourably on its simple Tory constancy than upon the philosophical coherence of minority rights (or vice versa). At the very least, the Tories are correct to say that we will not know this with any certainty for a long, long time.

NOTE

[1] See Robert Paul Wolff, Barrington Moore, and Herbert Marcuse, eds. *A Critique of Pure Tolerance* (Boston: Beacon Press, 1965).

BIBLIOGRAPHY

Adams, Michael. *Fire and Ice: The United States, Canada, and the Myth of Converging Values*. Toronto: Penguin Canada, 2003.

Ajzenstat, Janet. *The Political Thought of Lord Durham*. Montreal and Kingston: McGill-Queen's University Press, 1988.

Ajzenstat, Janet. *The Once and Future Canadian Democracy: An Essay in Political Thought*. Montreal and Kingston: McGill-Queen's University Press, 2003.

Ajzenstat, Janet, and Peter J. Smith, eds. *Canada's Origins: Liberal, Tory, or Republican?* Ottawa: Carleton University Press, 1995.

Ajzenstat, Janet, William D. Gairdner, Ian Gentles, and Paul Romney, eds. *Canada's Founding Debates*. Toronto: Stoddart, 1999; Toronto: University of Toronto Press, 2003.

Althusser, Louis. "Ideology and ideological state apparatuses." *"Lenin and Philosophy" and Other Essays*. New York: Monthly Review Press, 1971. 127–86.

Armour, Leslie. "Canadian philosophy: the nature and history of a discipline? A reply to Mr. Mathien." *Dialogue* 25 (1986): 67–82.

Armour, Leslie, and Elizabeth Trott. *The Faces of Reason: An Essay on Philosophy and Culture in English Canada, 1850–1950*. Waterloo: Wilfrid Laurier Press, 1981.

Armour, Leslie and Elizabeth Trott. "*The Faces of Reason* and its critics." *Dialogue* 25 (1986): 105-18.

Atkinson, A.B. *The Economics of Inequality*. Oxford: Clarendon Press, 1983.

Bakvis, Herman. *Federalism and the Organization of Political Life: Canada in Comparative Perspective*. Kingston: Institute of Intergovernmental Relations, 1981.

Barry, Brian. *Culture and Equality: An Egalitarian Critique of Multiculturalism*. Cambridge, MA: Harvard University Press, 2001.

Baxter-Moore, Nicolas, Terrance Carroll, and Roderick Church. *Studying Politics*. Toronto: Copp Clark Longman, 1994.

Beauchemin, Jacques. "What does it mean to be a Quebecer? Between self-preservation and openness to the other." *Québec: State and Society*. Ed. Alain-G. Gagnon. 3rd ed. Peterborough: Broadview Press, 2004. 17–32.

Beiner, Ronald, and Wayne Norman. *Canadian Political Philosophy: Contemporary Reflections*. Don Mills, ON: Oxford University Press Canada, 2001.

Bélanger, Claude. *Quebec History*. August 2004. Marianopolis College, Montreal, PQ. 21 September 2005. <http://www2.marianopolis.edu/quebechistory/index.htm>.

Berger, Thomas R. "Towards the regime of tolerance." *Political Thought in*

Canada. Ed. Stephen Brooks. Toronto: Irwin Publishing, 1984. 83–96.

Black, Naomi, Paula Boure, Gail Cuthbert Brandt, Beth Light, Wendy Mitchinson, and Alison Prentice. *Canadian Women: A History.* 2nd ed. Toronto: Harcourt Brace Canada, 1996.

Boldt, Menno. *Surviving as Indians: The Challenge to Self-Government.* Toronto: University of Toronto Press, 1993.

Bourassa, Henri. *The Spectre of Annexation and The Real Danger of National Disintegration.* Montreal: *Le Devoir,* 1912.

Brooks, Stephen, ed. *Political Thought in Canada.* Toronto: Irwin Publishing, 1984.

Brown, G.P. *Documents on the Confederation of British North America.* Toronto: McClelland and Stewart, 1969.

Brunet, Michel. "Trois dominantes de la pensée canadienne-française." *Études sur l'historie et la pensée des deux Canadas.* Montreal: Beauchemin, 1958.

Bullen, John. "The Ontario Waffle and the struggle for an independent socialist Canada: conflict within the NDP." *Interpreting Canada's Past: After Confederation.* Ed. J.M. Bumstead. Toronto: Oxford University Press, 1986. 430–52.

Bumstead, J.M. ed. *Interpreting Canada's Past: After Confederation.* Toronto: Oxford University Press, 1986.

Cairns, Alan. *Citizens Plus: Aboriginal Peoples and the Canadian State.* Vancouver: University of British Columbia Press, 2000.

Canada. Indian and Northern Affairs. *Report of the Royal Commission on Aboriginal Peoples.* Ottawa: Supply and Services, 1996.

Clark, S.D. *The Developing Canadian Community.* 2nd ed. Toronto: University of Toronto Press, 1968.

Cooper, Barry. "Western political consciousness." *Political Thought in Canada.* Ed. Stephen Brooks. Toronto: Irwin, 1984. 213–38.

Corbo, Claude, and Yvan Lamonde, eds. *Le rouge et le bleu: une anthologie de la pensée politique au Québec de la Conquête à la Révolution tranquille.* Montreal: Les Presses de l'Université de Montréal, 1999.

Creighton, Donald. *The Road to Confederation: The Emergence of Canada, 1863–1867.* Toronto: Macmillan, 1964.

Crick, Bernard. *The American Science of Politics: Its Origins and Conditions.* London: Routledge and Kegan Paul, 1959.

Curtis, James, and Edward Grabb. *Regions Apart: The Four Societies of Canada and the United States.* Toronto: Oxford University Press, 2005.

Dahl, Robert. "The behaviouralist approach in political science: epitaph for a monument to a successful protest." *The American Political Science Review* 55.4 (December 1961): 763–72.

Drury, Shadia. *Leo Strauss and the American Right.* New York: St. Martin's Press, 1997.

Drury, Shadia. *The Political Ideas of Leo Strauss.* New York: St. Martin's Press, 1988.

Dumont, Fernand. "De quelques obstacles à la prise de conscience chez les Canadiens français." *Le rouge et le bleu: une anthologie de la pensée politique au Québec de la Conquête à la Révolution tranquille.* Ed. Yvan Lamonde and Claude

Corbo. Montreal: Les Presses de l'Université de Montréal, 1999.

Dumont, Fernand. *Genèse de la société québécoise.* Montreal: Boréal, 1996.

Dunn, John. *The Politics of Socialism.* Cambridge: Cambridge University Press, 1984.

Eisenberg, Avigail. "When (if ever) are referendums on minority rights fair?" *Representation and Democratic Theory.* Ed. David Laycock. Vancouver: University of British Columbia Press, 2004. 3–22.

Fairfield, Paul, Ingrid Harris, and G.B. Madison. *Is There a Canadian Philosophy? Reflections on the Canadian Identity.* Ottawa: University of Ottawa Press, 2000.

Fanon, Franz. *The Wretched of the Earth.* New York: Grove Press, 1963.

Fierlbeck, Katherine, ed. *The Development of Political Thought in Canada: An Anthology.* Peterborough, ON: Broadview Press, 2005.

Flanagan, Thomas. *First Nations? Second Thoughts.* Montreal and Kingston: McGill-Queen's University Press, 2000.

Flanagan, Thomas, and Christopher Alcantana. *Individual Property Rights on Canadian Indian Reserves.* Vancouver: Fraser Institute, 2002.

Forbes, H.D. *Canadian Political Thought.* Toronto: University of Toronto Press, 1985.

Forbes, H.D. "Hartz-Horowitz at twenty: nationalism, toryism, and socialism in Canada and the United States." *Canadian Journal of Political Science* 2.20 (June 1987): 287–315.

Frideres, James. *Aboriginal Peoples in Canada.* Scarborough, ON: Prentice-Hall, 1998.

Frost, Catherine. "Getting to yes: people, practices, and the paradox of multicultural democracy." *Representation and Democratic Theory.* Ed. David Laycock. Vancouver: University of British Columbia Press, 2004. 48–64.

Frye, Northrop. *The Bush Garden: Essays on the Canadian Imagination.* Toronto: Anansi Press, 1971.

Gagnon, Alain-G., ed. *Québec: State and Society.* 3rd ed. Peterborough: Broadview Press, 2004.

Gagnon, Alain-G. "The role of intellectuals in Quebec." *Political Thought in Canada.* Ed. Stephen Brooks. Toronto: Irwin Publishing, 1984. 185–210.

Grant, George. *Lament for Nation.* 1965. Ottawa: Carleton University Press, 1982.

Grant, George. *Technology and Empire.* Toronto: Anansi Press, 1969.

Grant, George. *Technology and Justice.* Toronto: Anansi Press, 1986.

Habermas, Jurgen. *Lifeworld and System.* Trans. T. McCarthy. London: Polity Press, 1987. Vol. 2 of *The Theory of Communicative Action: A Critique of Functionalist Reason.* 2 vols. 1984–87.

Halévy, Elie. *The Birth of Methodism in England.* 1913. Trans. Bernard Semmel. Chicago: University of Chicago Press, 1971.

Hartz, Louis, ed. *The Founding of New Societies.* New York: Harcourt Brace, 1964.

Hartz, Louis. *The Liberal Tradition in America.* New York: Harcourt Brace, 1955.

Hendel, Charles. "The character of philosophy in Canada." *Philosophy in Canada: A Symposium.* Ed. John Irving. Toronto: University of Toronto Press, 1952.

Horowitz, Gad. *Canadian Labour in Politics.* Toronto: University of Toronto

Press, 1968.

Horowitz, Gad. "Conservatism, liberalism, and socialism in Canada: an inter-pretation." *Canadian Journal of Political Science* 32.2 (May 1966): 144–71.

Houde, Rolande, ed. *Histoire et philosophie au Québec.* Trois-Rivières: Éditions du Bien Publique, 1979.

Kellogg, Paul. "After left nationalism: the future of Canadian political econ-omy." *A World to Win.* Spec. issue of *Marxism* 2 (2004): 21–31.

Kymlicka, Will. *Multicultural Citizenship.* Oxford: Clarendon Press, 1995.

Kymlicka, Will. "The new debate over minority rights." *Canadian Political Philosophy: Contemporary Reflections.* Ed. Ronald Beiner and Wayne Norman. Don Mills, ON: Oxford University Press, 2001. 159–76.

Laclau, Ernesto, and Chantal Mouffe. *Hegemony and Socialist Strategy: Towards a Radical Democratic Politics.* London: Verso, 1985.

Lamonde, Yvan. *Historiographie de la philosophie au Québec, 1853-1970.* Montreal: Les Cahiers du Québec, 1972.

LaSelva, Samuel. *The Moral Foundations of Canadian Federalism.* Montreal and Kingston: McGill-Queen's University Press, 1996.

Laycock, David, ed. *Representation and Democratic Theory.* Vancouver: University of British Columbia Press, 2004.

Lévesque, René. *An Option for Quebec.* Toronto: McClelland and Stewart, 1968.

Little, J.L. *Borderland Religion: The Emergence of an English-Canadian Identity, 1792-1852.* Toronto: University of Toronto Press, 2004.

Lowi, Theodore. "The state in political science: how we become what we study." *The American Political Science Review* 86.1 (March 1992): 1–7.

MacIntyre, Alasdair. *After Virtue.* Notre Dame: University of Notre Dame Press, 1984.

Maclure, Jocelyne. "Narratives and counter-narratives of identity in Quebec." *Québec: State and Society.* Ed. Alain-G. Gagnon. 3rd ed. Peterborough: Broadview Press, 2004. 33–50.

Macpherson, C.B. *Democracy in Alberta: Social Credit and the Party System.* Toronto: University of Toronto Press, 1953.

Macpherson, C.B. *The Real World of Democracy.* Toronto: CBC Enterprises. 1983.

Mancke, Elizabeth. "Early modern imperial governance and the origins of Canadian political culture." *The Canadian Journal of Political Science* 32.1 (March 1999): 3–20.

Marcuse, Herbert, Barrington Moore, and Robert Paul Wolff, eds. *A Critique of Pure Tolerance.* Boston: Beacon Press, 1965.

Mardiros, Anthony. *William Irvine: The Life of a Prairie Radical.* Toronto: James Lorimer, 1979.

Martin, Ged. *Britain and the Origins of Canadian Confederation, 1937-67.* Vancouver: University of British Columbia Press, 1995.

McClung, Nellie. *In Times Like These.* Toronto: McLeod and Allen, 1915.

McLuhan, Marshall. *Understanding Media: The Extensions of Man.* New York: McGraw-Hill, 1964.

McRoberts, Kenneth, and Dale Posgate. *Quebec: Social Change and Political Crisis.*

Toronto: McCelland and Stewart, 1980.

Mellon, Hugh, and Martin Westmacott, eds. *Challenges to Canadian Federalism.* Scarborough: Prentice-Hall, 1998.

Miliband, Ralph. "The capitalist state: reply to N. Poulantzas." *New Left Review* 1.59 (January-February 1970): 67–78.

Mills, David. *The Concept of Loyalty in Upper Canada, 1784-1850.* Kingston and Montreal: McGill-Queen's University Press, 1988.

Monière, Denis. "Currents of nationalism in Quebec." *Political Thought in Canada.* Ed Stephen Brooks. Toronto: Irwin Publishing, 1984. 153–84.

Moore, Christopher. *1867: How the Fathers Made a Deal.* Toronto: McClelland and Stewart, 1997.

Morris, Aldon D., and Carol McClurg Mueller, eds. *Frontiers in Social Movement Theory.* New Haven: Yale University Press, 1992.

Morton, W.L. *The Critical Years: The Union of British North America, 1857-73.* Toronto: McClelland and Stewart, 1964.

Morton, W.L. *The Progressive Party in Canada.* Toronto: University of Toronto Press, 1950.

Morton, W.L. "The relevance of Canadian history." Presidential address to the Canadian Historical Association, Queen's University, 11 June 1960.

Muggeridge, John. "Grant's anguished conservatism." *George Grant in Process.* Ed. Larry Schmidt. Toronto: Anansi Press, 1978. 40–48.

Neill, Robin. *A New Theory of Value: The Canadian Economics of H.A. Innis.* Toronto: University of Toronto Press, 1972.

O'Brien, Rory, and Stella Theodoulou, eds. *Methods for Political Inquiry: The Discipline, Philosophy, and Analysis of Politics.* New Jersey: Prentice Hall, 1999.

O'Connor, James. *The Fiscal Crisis of the State.* New York: St. Martin's Press, 1973.

Offe, Claus. *The Contradictions of the Welfare State.* Ed. John Keane. Cambridge, MA: MIT Press, 1984.

Olling, R.D., and M.W. Westmacott, eds. *Perspectives on Canadian Federalism.* Scarborough: Prentice-Hall, 1988.

Panitch, Leo, ed. *The Canadian State: Political Economy and Political Power.* Toronto: University of Toronto Press, 1977.

Parkin, George. "The reorganization of the British Empire." *Canadian Political Thought.* Ed. H.D. Forbes. Toronto: Oxford University Press, 1985. 156–65.

Patterson, Annabel. *Early Modern Liberalism.* Cambridge: Cambridge University Press, 1997.

Pearson, Lester B. *Words and Occasions.* Toronto: University of Toronto Press, 1970.

Penner, Norman. *The Canadian Left: A Critical Analysis.* Scarborough: Prentice Hall Canada, 1977.

Plessis, Joseph-Octave. "Sermon on Nelson's victory in Aboukir." *Canadian Political Thought.* Ed. H.D. Forbes. Toronto: Oxford University Press, 1985. 2–9.

Poulantzas, Nicos. "The problem of the capitalist state." *New Left Review* 1.58 (November-December 1969): 67–78.

Przeworski, Adam, and John Sprague. *Paper Stones: A History of Electoral Socialism.*

Chicago: University of Chicago Press, 1986.

Putnam, Robert. *Bowling Alone: The Collapse and Revival of American Community.* New York: Simon and Schuster, 2000.

Quintin, Paul-André, and Claude Panaccio, eds. *Philosophie au Québec.* Montreal: Bellarmin, 1976.

Reimer, A. James. "George Grant: liberal, socialist, or conservative?" *George Grant in Process.* Ed. Larry Schmidt. Toronto: Anansi Press, 1978. 49–57.

Rioux, Marcel. *Quebec in Question.* Trans. James Boake. Toronto: James Lorimer, 1978.

Robertson, Neil, "Leo Strauss's Platonism." *Animus* 4 (1999). 21 September 2005 <http://www.swgc.mun.ca/animus/1999vol4/roberts4.htm>.

Rorty, Richard. *Achieving Our Country: Leftist Thought in Twentieth-Century America.* Cambridge, MA: Harvard University Press, 1998.

Said, Edward. *Culture and Imperialism.* New York: Knopf, 1993.

Said, Edward. *Orientalism.* New York: Pantheon Books, 1978.

Scott, Frank R. *Civil Liberties and Canadian Federalism.* Toronto: University of Toronto Press, 1959.

Semple, Neil. *The Lord's Dominion: The History of Canadian Methodism.* Montreal and Kingston: McGill-Queen's University Press, 1996.

Smiley, Donald. *The Federal Condition in Canada.* Toronto: McGraw-Hill Ryerson, 1987.

Smith, Goldwin, "The political destiny of Canada." *Canadian Political Thought.* Ed. H.D. Forbes. Toronto: Oxford University Press, 1985. 115–33.

Smith, Jennifer. "Intrastate federalism and confederation." *Political Thought in Canada.* Ed. Stephen Brooks. Toronto: Irwin Publishing, 1984. 258–77.

Sokal, Alan. "Transgressing the boundaries: towards a transformative hermeneutics of quantum gravity." *Social Text* (Spring/Summer 1996): 217–52.

Stewart, Gordon T. *The Origins of Canadian Politics: A Comparative Approach.* Vancouver: University of British Columbia Press, 1986.

Strachan, John. "On Church establishment." *Canadian Political Thought.* Ed. H.D. Forbes. Toronto: Oxford University Press, 1985. 10–17.

Taylor, Charles. *The Malaise of Modernity.* Concord, ON: Anansi Press, 1991.

Taylor, Charles. *Philosophical Papers I: Human Agency and Language.* Cambridge: Cambridge University Press, 1985.

Taylor, Charles. *Philosophical Papers II: Philosophy and the Human Sciences.* Cambridge: Cambridge University Press, 1985.

Taylor, Charles. *Reconciling the Solitudes: Essays on Canadian Federalism and Nationalism.* Ed. Guy Laforest. Montreal and Kingston: McGill–Queen's University Press, 1993.

Taylor, E.P. *Methodism and Politics, 1791-1851.* New York: Russell and Russell, 1975.

Tilly, Charles. *From Mobilization to Revolution.* New York: McGraw-Hill, 1978.

Trudeau, Pierre Elliott. *Federalism and the French Canadians.* Toronto: Macmillan, 1968.

Tully, James. *Strange Multiplicity: Constitutionalism in an Age of Diversity.* Cambridge University Press, 1995.

Tuohy, Carolyn Hughes. "Social policy: two worlds." *Governing Canada: Institutions and Public Policy*. Ed. Michael Atkinson. Toronto: Harcourt Brace Jovanovich, 1993.

Underhill, Frank. *In Search of Canadian Liberalism*. Toronto: Macmillan, 1960.

Waite, Peter. *The Life and Times of Confederation*. Toronto: University of Toronto Press, 1962.

Wearmouth, Robert F. *Methodism and the Working-Class Movements in England, 1800-1850*. Clifton, NJ: A.M. Kelly, 1972.

Wiseman, Nelson. "A note on 'Hartz-Horowitz at twenty': the case of French Canada." *Canadian Journal of Political Science* 21.4 (December 1988): 795–806.

Wiseman, Nelson. "Provincial political cultures." *Provinces: Canadian Provincial Politics*. Ed. Chris Dunn. Peterborough: Broadview Press, 1996. 21–62.

Woodcock, George, ed. *The Anarchist Reader*. Glasgow: Fontana Paperbacks, 1977.

Young, I.M. "Polity and group difference: a critique of the ideal of universal citizenship." *Ethics* 99.2 (1989): 250–74.

Young, Walter D. *Democracy and Discontent: Progressivism, Socialism, and Social Credit in the Canadian West*. Toronto: McGraw-Hill Ryerson, 1969.

INDEX

Panitch, Leo, *Canadian State, The*, 111
Papineau, Louis-Joseph, 11, 78, 123
   nationalism, 122
   "Six Counties Address," 60
Parent, Etienne, 124
Parkin, George, 53
Parti Canadien, 122
Parti Patriote, 122
   English Canadian members, 123
   Irish Catholic community support, 123
Parti pris, 135
Parti Rouges, 124
"the Patrons of Industry," 103
"Peace, Order, and Good
   Government," 11
Pearson, Lester B., 10, 62
Penner, Norman, 104–05
Petro-Canada, 82
"philosophical idealism," 23
philosophy, 24
   "Canadian" approaches to, 22
   postmodernism, 33
"Philosophy in Canada" (symposium), 22
Plato, 30
Plessis, Joseph-Octave, 121
pluralism, 6, 143
political culture
   fragment theory, 13–14, 87–92
political economy, 24, 36, 81
"political philosophy," 24–25
political science, 24–25, 71, 77
   institutional (formal-legal)
     approach, 26
   mainstream, 31
   Marxist studies, 29
political science departments, 28
populism, 53, 73–74, 107
   agrarian, 14, 46, 101, 103–06
   anti-populism, 69
"post-Hegelian idealism," 23
post-structuralism, 33
postcolonialism, 31, 34
postmodernism, 16, 21, 32–34, 37, 113,
   115, 148
   impact on Marxist thought, 111
   literary theory, 33
Potash Corporation of Saskatchewan, 75
Poulantzas, Nicos, 110
Pour la patrie (Tardival), 128
poverty, 29, 62
   relation to American capitalist
     expansion, 36
power, nature of, 33–34

prairie populism. *See* populism
Prairie provinces, 103
   American immigrants, 95
Principles of Political Economy (Mill), 24
private property, 75, 106, 112
Progressive Conservative Party, 74, 76
Progressives, 107
prohibition, 52
Protestantism, 48–49
psychoanalysis, 31
psychological and political
   alienation, 29
psychology of political oppression, 135
Putnam, Robert, "Bowling Alone," 114

quantitative research methodology, 27,
   30, 33
"quasi-party" politics, 74, 106
Quebec, 15, 37, 61, 63, 88, 133, 149
   autonomy, 137
   foreign and English Canadian
     capital, 129
   French Canadian capital, 129
   immigration levels, 130
   industrialization, 128
   involvement at federal level, 145
   liberal rather than nationalist reform,
     144–45
   Padlock Act, 63
   progressive labour legislation, 130
   referenda, 37
   sovereignty, 16
   special status for, 136
   "technocratic" class, 128, 130
Quebec Act, 121
Quebec intelligentsia, 129
Quebec nationalism, 20, 119, 129, 131,
   143–44. *See also* French Canadian
   nationalism
   neo-nationalism, 130
la québécité, 137
Quebecois identity, 131, 135
Quiet Revolution, 37, 128–29, 135, 137

race and racism, 29, 97, 113
radical approaches (or radicalism),
   28–29, 31
   in Canada, 68, 101, 104
   market-based political radicalism, 75
   radical feminism, 113
   radical (fragments), 88
radio and television technology, 79
railroads, 103, 105

social norms
  state involvement in, 76
social philosophy, 29
Social Planning for Canada, 108
social reform, 62
social relationships, 136
social science, 33
  quantitative research methodology,
    27, 33
social tolerance. *See* tolerance
social welfare policy. *See* Canada's
  welfare state
socialism, 16, 94, 102, 135, 140. *See also*
  the Left
  Canada, 76, 89
  doctrinal divisions, 104
  United States, 87–89
socialist feminism, 112–13
Socialist Party of Canada, 104
"Sokal hoax," 34
Sources of the Self, The (Taylor), 39
sovereignty, 77–78, 82. *See also*
  nationalism
  in Canadian political thought, 77
  divided, 60
  legal *vs.* political, 82
  Levesque's argument for, 145
  Quebec, 16, 37
Soviet Union, 112
  demise of, 32
  liberalization, 114
St. Lawrence River, 73
Stamp Act, 64
"staples" or natural resources, 36, 54
state ownership, 109
state sovereignty. *See* sovereignty
Stewart, Gordon T., 91
Strachan, John, 11, 48–51
Strauss, Leo, 30
"strong state" tradition in Canada, 50, 65,
    71–72, 92
"structural functionalist" approach, 28
survivance, 124, 127
Suzuki, David, 113
Syllabus of Errors (Pope Pious IX), 126
systems analysis, 28, 36

Tammany Hall, 79
Tardival, Jules-Paul, *Pour la patrie*, 128
tariffs, 103
Taylor, Charles, 7, 38, 133, 137,
    145–46, 154
  "Atomism," 136

on equality, 138
Malaise of Modernity, 39
Sources of the Self, The, 39
"What's wrong with negative
  liberty," 136
Taylor, E. P., 94
"technocratic" class in Quebec, 128, 130
technology, 53–54, 56
  McLuhan's "double dialectic," 55
television, 54
temperance, 76
Thatcher, Margaret, 67
"third option," 82
Thomism, 128
tolerance, 63, 157, 159
  United Church, 98
Toryism, 13, 17, 45–46, 50, 53–57, 69,
    87–90, 92, 98, 152, 155, 159. *See*
    also British colonial legacy
  American rejection of, 47
  deference, 51
  in differentiating Canada from
    U.S., 88
  fit with Catholic Church, 121
  French Catholic population and,
    49–50
  and imperialism, 156
  Tory / left-wing coalition, 68, 77, 81
  Tory collectivism, 51
  Tory values, 76
  tradition (respect for the past), 8, 49,
    51, 58, 83
traditional (Christian) values, 45
traditional cultural values, 38
Treatises of Government (Locke), 58
Trudeau, Pierre, 7, 10, 109, 135, 144–45
Truth, 30, 33
Tully, James, 39
Turner, F. J.
  "frontier thesis," 35

UFA, 52, 104, 106
ultramontane nationalism, 119,
    125–28, 144
Underhill, Frank, 60–61, 73
Understanding Media (McLuhan), 54
unemployment insurance, 62
United Church, 96–97
  importance in Canada, 93
  tolerance, 98
United Farmers Association, 74
United Farmers' Cooperative Company
  (UFCC), 104

United Farmers of Alberta (UFA), 52,
104, 106
United Farmers' Organization (UFO),
104
United Grain Growers (UGG), 52
United Kingdom, 8, 70, 94, 104
United States, 12–14, 26–27, 63, 78, 104.
See also headings beginning
American
civil war, 61
division between Church and State,
92, 98
doctrine of manifest destiny, 70
evangelical, fundamental
Protestantism, 76, 93, 95
free enterprise capitalism, 70
Free Methodists, 94
industrial capitalism, 79
intellectual polarization, 35
Methodism, 49, 94
nationalism, 6
plurality of liberalisms, 68
political thought (*See* American
political thought)
populist alliance movements, 53
radicalism, 36 (*See also* the Left)
secession, 48
Social Gospel Movement, 97
socialism, 87–89
state involvement in moral issues, 76
War of Independence, 94
universal suffrage, 69, 96
universalism, 90, 146
universities, 10, 23. *See also* academic
discourse
expansion of, 28
Upper Canada, 58
loyalty to Crown, 48
urban industrial workers, 15, 94, 106

Valpy, Michael, 11
"value gap," 12. *See also* Canadian /
American difference
"Vienna School," 27
Vietnam War, 29, 36
violence
tolerance for, 6
virtue, 30
Voice of Women, 112

"Waffle Manifesto," 109
Waltzer, Michael, 80
War of 1812, 94

Watkins Report, 81
Wealth of Nations, The (Smith), 24
Weimar Republic, 27
welfare liberalism, 16, 87
Wesleyan sect, 94
Western Canada, 73
development of, 62, 74
market liberalism, 68
Western Labour Conference, 106
"What's wrong with negative liberty"
(Taylor), 136
Who Owns Canada?, 108
Winnipeg Declaration (1944), 108
Winnipeg General Strike, 106
Wiseman, Nelson, 75, 123
Wolff, Robert Paul, 157
Women's Christian Temperance
Union, 112
Women's Liberation movements, 29
women's movement, 112
women's suffrage, 52, 97
Wood, Henry Wise, 74
guild socialism, 52, 106
Woodcock, George, 114–15
Woodsworth, J. S., 10, 96, 107–08
workforce, 15, 94, 106, 110. *See also*
agricultural producers